LIGHT FROM DARKE:

SEVENTY ILLUMINATING DEVOTIONS

REG DARKE

Published by:

***HAYES PRESS Publisher**, Resources & Media,*

The Barn, Flaxlands

Royal Wootton Bassett

Swindon, SN4 8DY

United Kingdom

www.hayespress.org

Unless otherwise indicated, all Scripture quotations are from the Revised Version Bible (Public Domain).

If you enjoy reading this book and/or others in the series, we would really appreciate it if you could just take a couple of minutes to leave a brief review where you purchased it.

ONE: THE GOD OF SMALL THINGS

Christians, above all others, should be able to appreciate the great importance of small things, made and used so much by our Creator. It is interesting to notice in Scripture the element of smallness in many of the divine miracles. An example is the manna: "there, on the surface of the wilderness, was a small round substance, *as* fine as frost on the ground" (Exodus 16:14), typical no doubt of the Bread of Life.

In Elijah's day, a little cake was made for him by a widow from her small resources of a little oil and a handful of flour. She thought her gesture would empty the bin and the jug for good, but her faithful willingness resulted in the divine promise: "The bin of flour shall not be used up, nor shall the jar of oil run dry, until the day the LORD sends rain ..." (1 Kings 17:14). Elijah, the widow, and her son fed from the same jar and bin many days (v.15). The testimony of a little girl led to the miraculous cleansing of Naaman the leper (2 Kings 5); the sacrifice of a little boy enabled the Lord Jesus to feed miraculously more than five thousand people with five barley loaves and two small fish (John 6:9).

God has made a brain for us, a comparatively small organ of the human body whose function and complexity confound the greatest of minds. Scientists tell us that the brain has ten million nerve cells for recording things we learn. "The information travels inside us at speeds of up to 300 miles per hour over a network of nerve fibres 100,000 miles long" states one report. We could go on to write of the miracle of the tiny dew drop, the blade of grass, the wheat kernel, the ant; all wonderful examples of God's purpose in small things. But certain spiders deserve special mention for they were recently responsible for creating a phenomenon in the U.S.A. which puzzled many people. When they wish to migrate, families of spiders weave huge webs, some 20 feet long, and use them to float to their destinations.

In a similar way, Agur the son of Jakeh was impressed by the wisdom of "four things which are little on the earth, but they are exceedingly wise: The ants are a people not strong, yet they prepare their food in the summer; The rock badgers are a feeble folk, yet they make their homes in the crags; the locusts have no king, yet they all advance in ranks. The spider skillfully grasps with its hands, and it is in kings' palaces" (Proverbs 30:24-28). We, too, may gain much wisdom in considering God's ways in taking up very small things for the progress of His great purposes.

TWO: MY WORK IS FOR THE KING (PART ONE)

There is a man in the Bible who lost his life through jealousy and rebellion. If his sights had been raised to the devotional level of his descendants, he would have been a happy, contented man of vision. Our contrast is between Korah, whose death is recorded in Numbers 16, and the sons of Korah for whom Psalm 45 was written probably 400 years later. Korah's heart was filled with haughtiness, discontent, ambition and bitterness which led to such tragic circumstances that his name is linked with two of history's worst reprobates, Cain and Balaam, in the short letter by Jude in the New Testament.

But the sons of Korah sing from hearts that are not only filled but bubbling over with gracious, beautiful, loving; joyful things concerning the king, for that is the meaning of "goodly" in Psalm 45:1. If only Korah had said, "My work is for a king" (v.1 Revised Version margin); what a different outcome there could have been. But he had things in wrong perspective; his sights were not raised above his discontent and selfish ambitions. The sad conclusion is that his work was for himself.

The sight which greeted Nehemiah when he arrived at Jerusalem after a wearying journey of months, would have broken the spirit of many other great men. Untouched rubble, burned gates, broken wall, and a dispirited people. Chaos in contrast to the orderly array of the palace and environs of Shushan, which he had left. Instead of despair or defeat, he met the enormity of the task in the spirit of the words: "My work is for the King". Before he ventured out from Shushan he had spent time in the King's presence weeping, mourning, fasting, praying, and pleading with Him to remember the promise to His people if they returned to the land (Nehemiah 1:9).

It is no surprise, then, to hear from such a man these words: "... the hand of my God which was good upon me ... then they set their hands to this good work (Nehemiah 2:18) ... So we built the wall ... So we laboured in the work; and half of the men held the spears from daybreak till the stars appeared (Nehemiah 4:6,21) ... Indeed, I continued the work (5:16) ... So the wall was finished ... in fifty-two days" (Nehemiah 6:15). Against mockings, tauntings, threats, and devious plots by the enemy, Nehemiah and his people completed a memorable task against almost insurmountable odds. They climbed their Mount Everest and reached the top. Their flag might have said, "Excelsior", but instead it read, "My work is for the King". Let us then rejoice! Let our hearts overflow with joy, grace, beauty - the "goodly things"! The Lord reigns! My work is for the King!

THREE: MY WORK IS FOR THE KING (PART TWO)

A missionary to China wrote home to his parents outlining his grim prison ordeal. The details were not pleasant, but each paragraph ended with the triumphant words: "The Lord reigns". This was the way he kept things in perspective. He recognized with the Psalmist: "...my work is for a king". When our earliest Christian forbears were challenged to declare: "Caesar is king", they replied: "Jesu Christos Rex", Jesus Christ is King! Their bold assertion led to death in the arena, torture at the stake, or being stretched mercilessly on the rack. Instead of slowing down progress in the gospel and the truth, it seemed to accelerate it, to the ire of their Roman tormentors. These Christian disciples did not need to declare "my work is for the King", for their very lives proclaimed it.

What of today's spiritual royal family? Those who comprise the little flock, to whom was given the kingdom (Luke 12:32) - those proclaimed by Peter as a royal priesthood (1 Peter 2:9)? We are not thrown into prison, tortured or massacred because we pledge our allegiance to Jesus as King. Yet, it is still essential that we recognize, and others know, that our work is for the King. It is so easy to be discouraged and depressed by society's response to the word of God; easy for apathy, malaise to replace our former zeal; to lose faith in the effort of distributing leaflets, and in the personal work of sharing Christ with a desperate, needy world. Perhaps we need to convince ourselves on a personal basis that "my work is for the King".

On the positive side, there are Christians who cheerfully fill jobs which need more grace than others. Nursing care, for example, in the home, in hospital, or at geriatric centres, where very unpleasant tasks have to be undertaken. How depressing and discouraging such work can be if it is not undertaken in the spirit of "my work is for the King". This realization, with all its encouragement, enables us to bring our lives into perspective, with the added help in these words of Paul: "Therefore, my beloved brethren, be steadfast, immovable, always abounding in the work of the Lord, knowing that your labor is not in vain in the Lord" (1 Corinthians 15:58).

FOUR: TOO HARD FOR THE LORD? (PART ONE)

Christians can become discouraged and even downright pessimistic over the possibility of wayward children of God being restored to a life of fruitful service. They forget the bright ray of hope which the Lord Jesus provides in telling of the father's eagerness to forgive his repentant prodigal son. The words: "his father saw him and had compassion, and ran and fell on his neck and kissed him" (Luke 15:20) reflect also the eagerness of our heavenly Father to forgive and restore His repentant ones.

"There is forgiveness with You", cried David (Psalm 130:4). "... Return to the Lord, and He will have mercy ... and to our God, for He will abundantly pardon", said Isaiah (Isaiah 55:7). "Her sins which are many are forgiven", declared the Lord Jesus (Luke 7:47). "If we confess our sins, He is faithful and just to forgive us our sins, and to cleanse us from all unrighteousness", proclaimed John (1 John 1:9). What clearer evidence do we need than these remarkable scriptural assurances to confirm God's willingness to forgive and restore?

Proof that backsliders can be restored was vividly portrayed at the bedside of a dying Christian. His father was a godly man who had served his generation well; the son was a baptized disciple but he left the church after a gradual drift away from spiritual things through family tragedy and discouragement. "The seat in the assembly circle is empty long before the person leaves" is a cryptic, yet true statement, and it was so in this man's case. When he left God's people, the drift away from the Lord was most perceptible. He was in Christ, but he was not enjoying the abiding life of fruitfulness. His occupation was the dangerous one of a firefighter, but it did not seem to occur to him that each day he was but a step away from death; that there was the daily risk of being ushered into the divine presence with so many things unreconciled with His Master. It was that insidious enemy of cancer which proved to be the blessing in disguise. Doctors and nurses could not help any more and they sent him home to die.

That was when the message came and we paid our memorable visit. He was happy to be reminded of the love of the Lord Jesus, to be assured that failure and folly could be forgiven. He asked us to read to him from his father's Bible. It was a well-worn, well-read, well-marked book; a cherished heritage. We prayed together, and we returned the following night at his request. That proved to be the last occasion, for he later lapsed into a coma and passed away. Another wanderer had come home confessing: "Father, I have sinned against heaven, and in your sight: I am no more worthy to be called your son" (Luke 15:21). He had known forgiveness and acceptance. It was a joy to give such a testimony at his funeral.

FIVE: TOO HARD FOR THE LORD? (PART TWO)

Speaking of things that seem too hard, what shall we say of Peter, the tempted, failing disciple who betrayed his Lord? Tears of repentance led to a mighty restoration. God used him to bring thousands to the Lord on the day of Pentecost. "And when you have returned to me, strengthen your brethren" (Luke 22:32); Peter fulfilled this desire of his Lord in a very practical way. In contrast Paul lamented over Demas who "has forsaken me, having loved this present world" (2 Timothy 4:10). The end of Demas' life is hidden from us, but we can only think of it with sadness. There are many known to us who have drifted away from the Lord and His things. Are we praying for them? Assuring them of our prayers? Sending them a booklet or a little message from the Lord? Seeking their restoration in the spirit of the eagerness of our forgiving God? This is a service for God which needs wisdom, compassion; but it is an important work for there is a life at stake, a life that is being wasted.

A good start is to tell the wayward ones that we are praying for their restoration; let us tell them also of God's cry to the Israelite who had shamefully left the Lord for a life of sin. "Will you not from this time cry to Me, 'My Father, You are the guide of my youth?' (Jeremiah 3:4). It is almost as though God is teaching the backslider, the Israelite idol worshipper, how to pray, by putting into his mouth these wonderful words of pleading and restoration, "My Father, You are the guide of my youth". This might well be the acknowledgement of all our hearts.

Dr. Robert Morrison, medical missionary to China, was a living testimony to a Christian mother's ceaseless prayers for her two wayward sons. While she remained in Scotland one son went to the USA, became a heavy drinker of alcohol, and a mocker of Christians. He would wait for the congregation to leave an evangelical church in Chicago and would taunt them with his offers of alcohol. He was considered a hopeless case. But the mother's prayers, and the Spirit's pleading, brought him under the conviction of sin. One night he was awakened out of sleep, and as a trembling sinner he came to Christ.

He became one of God's good men, and subsequently returned home to convey to his mother the good news of her answered prayers for him. Overjoyed, Mrs Morrison invited her son to join with her in continued prayer for the son Robert, also a wayward lad. Unknown to the praying couple, Robert was brought under conviction on the deck of a ship in the China Sea. God caused him to review his mother's Christian influence on him as a boy and her continual prayers for his salvation. The Holy Spirit brought him to a realization of his need of Christ and he was born again. Returning to Scotland, he gave himself to the study of the Scriptures and medicine, and he dedicated his life to China as a medical missionary. "Is anything too hard for the Lord?" (Genesis 18:14).

SIX: THE GOD OF THE UNEXPECTED

Christians are startled when the Lord works in a way which is opposite to what they expect. We get into a rut, and often we follow a ritual of expectancy which allows for no change; then suddenly we wake up and find His word being fulfilled: "For My thoughts are not your thoughts, nor are your ways My ways, says the LORD" (Isaiah 55:8).

Did you know that our God is the God of the paradox? In the days of the Lord people were amazed when a man was healed and his sins were forgiven. "We have seen strange things today!", they said (Luke 5:26). We get our word paradox from this word "strange". The Lord did something contrary to human expectation, something extraordinary, and people were gripped by amazement. Some years ago, a single verse of poetry was found written on the wall of a room in a mental hospital. It was not written by the author, for the words were first penned more than three centuries before. And today this verse forms part of a beautiful hymn which Christians delight to sing.

"Could we with ink the ocean fill,

And were the skies of parchment made;

Were every stalk on earth a quill,

And every man a scribe by trade;

To write the love of God above

Would drain the ocean dry;

Nor could the scroll contain the whole.

Though stretched from sky to sky."

These words were said to have been composed by a Jewish rabbi, and God has allowed them to be preserved to console redeemed hearts, and to bring sinners to Christ. They were quoted one night by a preacher, and a derelict who heard them phoned to ask if it could possibly be true that God would love a wicked sinner like himself. The message of love was preached over the phone, and the listening sinner was saved. Strange? Yes. Paradoxical? Only to us, for "God moves in a mysterious way His wonders to perform".

SEVEN: WHAT EVER HAPPENED TO THOSE SHIELDS?

They were of immense value, and they hung for years on the walls of Solomon's sumptuous palace in the woods. There were 300 shields in all, and each weighed three "minas" (about 10 pounds, according to 1 Kings 10:17). They were made of fine gold, and at today's value one of those shields would be worth about $160,000 dollars. Three hundred shields, then, represented a fortune of approximately $50 million dollars. The golden shields might have been to Solomon a symbol of divine protection. The Hebrew word used here for shield is the same as that used in God's promise to Abram. "Do not be afraid, Abram: I am your shield, your exceedingly great reward" (Genesis 15:1). The meaning of the word is strength, protection, defence against an enemy.

Solomon's reign ended in decline and there was no improvement in the spiritual condition of Judah during the reign of his son, Rehoboam. "Now Judah did evil in the sight of the Lord, and they provoked Him to jealousy with their sins which they committed, more than all that their fathers had done." (1 Kings 14:22). Their evil included the worshipping of idols in secluded places, the tolerance of homosexual acts, and many other abominations learned from the nations around. It is no surprise therefore to know of the ease with which Egypt's king Shishak invaded Jerusalem, robbing the Temple of its treasures and stripping the walls of Solomon's house of its 300 shields of fine gold.

Where were the guardians of the king's domain while this was going on? What happened to the shields? Taken back to Egypt, no doubt, and used for the boastful claim of the enemy's prowess over a weakened people of God. And what did Rehoboam do? Replace the shields? Yes, but not with fine gold. He had shields made of copper, and they did not fill the empty place on the walls of the king's house, but were kept in the chamber of the guards. There is no record of their active use against an enemy (1 Kings 14:25-28); and no attempt appears to have been made to recover the original shields. Such was the debilitated physical and spiritual health of the king and his people.

There must be a lesson in this for those who belong to the Israel of God today (Galatians 6:16). Our battles are spiritual, and are against the hosts of wickedness guided by God's arch-enemy, Satan. Our shields are the visible testimony to our faith in a living Lord who is able to keep us, protect us, guard us. How is this possible? By living for Him through the power of His word and the help of the Spirit.

Are our shields, the symbols of our trust in God, on display? Or have they been torn down by the enemy? Have they been replaced by something inferior which we keep handy if needed? The king of Egypt is an illustration of Satan in his control of society - "the whole world lies under the sway of the evil one" (1 John 5:19). By subtle attractions, and keeping us preoccupied with things material, he is endeavouring to break down our dependence on the Lord. He wants to deprive us of our benefits in Christ If he can snatch away our faith, our joy, our loyalty to the Truth; if he can encourage us to neglect prayer, assembly gatherings, spiritual exercises, distributing leaflets, caring for a young people's class, and reading the word; he will replace these things of eternal value with those of less importance. It will not be long then before it is evident that he has captured our shield of fine gold.

It is so easy for spiritual anaemia to afflict us all in these demanding days with their tension and pressure. Instead of being a people capable of doing exploits, we can quickly deteriorate into a people interested only in doing a minimum. What happened to Solomon's shields is not now of great importance; but we should know about our own shield. Is it in its place? Have I checked lately? Has it been displaced? What is filling that gap on the wall? Serious questions for us all to answer.

EIGHT: LORD, DON'T YOU CARE?

"Lord, don't you care?" It was the cry of a distraught woman unable to cope with the responsibilities of the home. It was a cry for help, for relief from the pressures and tensions at hand. It was an appeal coming from a conscientious, hard-working person. Many today can relate to her experience. The questioning cry did not pass unheeded, for the Lord Jesus was in that warm, friendly home of Martha and Mary at Bethany when the incident happened.

His quiet conversation with Mary was suddenly interrupted when Martha entered the room to express her anxious concern. Martha, that strong, godly woman, who made service to others a priority in her life, had found herself overwhelmed and was at breaking point. She loved the Lord, and delighted to welcome Him into the home, but on this particular visit the task of preparing the meal seemed greater than normal. Perhaps the sickness of Lazarus, the burden of caring for him, had taken its toll. Whatever the cause, the effect was seen in her dramatic outburst. "Lord, do you not care that my sister has left me to serve alone?" (Luke 10:40). She knew that Mary had been sitting adoringly at His feet, hanging on His every word. Mary was enjoying the good things, spiritual, while Martha was preparing the good things, natural.

With this there was nothing basically wrong. It is a balance which must become part of all our lives. We must all find time to sit at His feet to enjoy those quiet times of communion with Him, hearing His voice in the Word. Such meditations enable us to "grow in the grace and knowledge of our Lord and Saviour

Jesus Christ" (2 Peter 3:18). The mundane things of home and business life must still be handled on their regular basis. It is when things get sadly out of balance that we find ourselves frustrated, tense, and crying out our complaint as Martha did: "Lord, do you not care ... therefore tell her to help me". This is when we can sympathize with Martha, not forgetting that we need a word from the Lord.

In the now silent room the Lord turns from Mary to her sister. ""Martha, Martha, you are worried and troubled about many things. But one thing is needed, and Mary has chosen that good part, which will not be taken away from her" (vv. 41,42). This was not a rebuke, but rather the calming of a very upset person. The tone is kindly as He gives His full attention to this dear woman's distress. Those eyes of love looked into the besieged mind of Martha and saw how she was being pulled in all directions, mentally and emotionally. Where peace should be reigning there was discord; joy was replaced by tears and in her despair and distress she cried out. Thankfully she called for help from One who could give it. He brought things into perspective with His kindly word.

Whatever the Lord meant by "one thing is needed", it was obviously the opposite to what Martha was doing. She needed to change her programme; no more rushing here and there, wearing herself out by being over-occupied with the demands of life. The Lord in His wisdom described her situation as being "worried and troubled about many things", and He seeks to guide away from this upsetting environment to the "good part" which Mary had chosen.

If Christ is given anything but prime place then life becomes unbalanced. It is when we allow the circumstances and demands of life to oust His things, the things of the Spirit, the things associated with His Word, that we find that we cannot cope. So the pressures build up, the cares increase, and we find ourselves pulled and stretched by circumstances in all directions at once. Then follow the uncontrolled tears, the turmoil of mind and body, the emotional stress, the lack of sleep, the irritability, and the decline in spiritual interests. And the cry: "Lord, do You not care?"

Of course He cares! In the time of the storm on the lake, the disciples forgot momentarily His nearness, His deity, His power, and in their distress they cried: "Teacher, do you not care ...?" (Mark 4:38). Of course He cared, and instantly He came to their rescue! Peace followed, and a restoring of faith and joy in Him. Even David thought he had been wholly deserted when troubles forced him to flee to the cave for prayer and meditation. "Look", he says," ... no man cares for my soul" (Psalm 142:4). But the Lord cared; as he cried his anguished prayer the Lord was there with him and listening. The same One who walked with him through the valley of the shadow was with him in the cave. Jehovah Shammah, the Lord is there!

At no time must we doubt the presence of the Lord with us. Daily we must claim His promise: "Let your conduct be without covetousness; be content with such things as you have. For He Himself has said, "I will never leave you nor forsake you" (Hebrews 13:5). We should avoid letting financial matters come between ourselves and the Lord. He knows all about our circumstances; He knows the end from the beginning. "Let your gentleness (sweet reasonableness) be known to all men. The Lord is at hand" (Philippians 4:5). That word "gentleness" ("forbearance" in older versions) has been translated as "not demanding your lawful rights", knowing that the Lord is near to balance out the deficiencies. Another reminder of the Lord's presence. Dare we forget His promise to the disciples as He prepared to leave them knowing that they would pass through perilous times: "... and lo, I am with you always, even to the end of the age" (Matthew 28:20).

"At the blest mercy-seat

Pleading for me,

My feeble faith looks up,

O Lord, to Thee;

Help me the cross to bear,

Thy wondrous love declare,

Some song to raise, or prayer,

Something for Thee".

NINE: FROM THE GUTTER TO GLORY

My friend was a wastrel. But what he was, and what he became, are two different things. He reminded me of God's description of certain men He called to further His work in the early days of the Testimony. "God chose the foolish ... the weak ... and the base" (1 Corinthians 1:26-31). They were the base, the dregs of humanity. Strong and uncomplimentary words to say the least, but the meanings are borne out from the Greek. The Greek word for base is 'agenes', meaning unborn, uncreated, of no family, low born; Their genes (a word used greatly by scientists today), the means by which inherited characteristics of individuals are transmitted, were very much suspect. All because of sin, unquestionably. Yet through the power of the gospel an "unborn" sinner can be transformed into a "born again" saint. Amazing grace!

For my friend to lie dead drunk in the gutter was commonplace. He could not have gone any lower. Then he heard the good news that Christ Jesus came into the world to save sinners, and he was gloriously saved. The song of the drunkard was now changed to a hymn which he whistled and sang at every opportunity. This was a favourite verse of a hymn:

"From sinking sand He lifted me;

With tender Hand He lifted me;

From shades of night to plains of light,

Oh, praise His Name! He lifted me".

Every house in the small town where he had been known as a drunkard received from his hand a gospel leaflet. Most Saturday nights he would walk up and down the theatre queues distributing his tracts. It was a joy to sit with him on the occasion of the breaking of the bread. He valued greatly the holy priesthood service of God's people, and it never ceased to be a marvel to him that he had been chosen to participate in such a noble service. In the giving of thanks he would shed copious tears of devotion and appreciation for the Man of Calvary; and he would sob out his worship to the God of glory. We rarely witness such a scene today.

My friend might not have been chosen to be among the noble, the mighty, the wise of this world. But he was chosen, saved, and called by God; and he was not only a member of the royal family of heaven, but part of the royal priesthood of earth (see 1 Peter 2:9). Similar to Mephibosheth in some of life's circumstances, the brother of whom I write is now in the Presence of the King. From Lo-debar (see 2 Samuel 9) to the eternal banqueting house where flies the banner of eternal love! His experience is a sound lesson to us all to forget the world with all its fame, and rejoice that our names are "written in heaven" (Luke 10:20). God does the calling. To Him be the glory.

TEN: SECRETS OF THE FUTURE

There is nothing new under the sun, and for thousands of years people have resorted to horoscopes to provide answers to the "riddle of life". Horoscopers were to be found in Egypt, Babylon, and Canaan, and they had their links with the magicians, enchanters, wizards, and the sorcerers (see Isaiah 47:12-13). It is startling to find, therefore, in our "age of enlightenment", that millions of people still read and believe in things like horoscopes. Some are so dependent upon the daily predictions of the star-gazers that they have become addicted.

It was once claimed that in three European countries 50% to 75% of the adult populations read horoscopes. In the western world, hundreds of newspapers and websites carry horoscope readings. As fear, confusion, discontent, and uncertainty increase, so will intensify the desire of many people to reach out to the unseen and the unknown for solutions to their daily problems. They will continue to reject the Bible and embrace a book on the signs of the heavens; deaf ears will be turned to words of assurance from the Son of God, but they will listen intently to the doubtful predictions of the star-gazers. God once accused Babylon of giving itself over to pleasures, dwelling carelessly, and relying on her enchantments and sorceries. Then He warned: "You are wearied in the multitude of your counsels; Let now the astrologers, the stargazers, and the monthly prognosticators stand up and save you from what shall come upon you" (Isaiah 47:13).

History looks like repeating itself if modern man continues to rely on the almanack, clairvoyance, teacup readings, tarot cards, horoscopes, and the magic of our day; not forgetting even more sinister things such as witchcraft, the occult, and the like. We should be concerned about friends, acquaintances, and people generally who dabble in these dangerous systems, seeking to bring before them the need for knowing the power and joy of Christ in their lives. Paul confronted the occult in his day, and through the Name of the Lord Jesus he dealt effectively with it so that in one case a girl was benefited, and converted men brought their books on the magical arts and publicly burned them (Acts 16:18; 19:18-20).

There is a great difference between astronomy and astrology. The first deals with celestial bodies, their size and motions; the second purports to show the influence of the stars and planets on events and persons. Astronomy is a recognized science; astrology is not. There is no scientific basis to astrology, it is a superstition which interests the unwary, the gullible, and the insecure. It is a system which entices people to trust in the predictions of men, and to link their lives with things created, the stars and planets, rather than the Creator who made them. It provides a daily crutch for those who seem to lack the confidence to make decisions for themselves.

Men and women need the Lord to plan for them for He alone knows the future. Instead of seeking their answers from astrology, which is basically an escape from reality, they should turn to Him who is able to remove their fears and uncertainties about the future. Man is in the dark because of sin; this is responsible for his dilemma, and his answer is to be found in forgiveness through the shed blood of Christ and not through the stars and planets. Christians, too, need to be alerted to the dangers of reading and discussing things like horoscopes. It is yet another subtle way the enemy has of drawing us away from the Lord. There are many superstitions, apparently innocent, which sometimes trap the unwary.

For example, "touch wood" has its origin with the mistaken belief that touching relics of the cross would provide protection from danger; so people hundreds of years ago actually carried on their persons what were supposed to be genuine pieces of the cross of Calvary. Black cats, broken mirrors, salt over the shoulder, walking around ladders, are all connected with the same source as the original enchanters and soothsayers.

Nebuchadnezzar discovered that the wisdom of God found in Daniel and his friends was ten times better than all the magicians and enchanters in his realm (Daniel 1:20). The Christian's approach to this question is found in the wise words of Daniel to the same king. "The secret which the king has demanded, the wise men, the astrologers, the magicians, and the soothsayers cannot declare to the king. But there is a God in heaven who reveals secrets ..." (Daniel 2:27,28). We are on the side of God.

ELEVEN: JEHOVAH ROPHEKA AND JEHOVAH SHALOM

Jehovah Ropheka

Not many things disrupt family life more than serious illness. It seems to cast a pall over everything. Rest and sleep become disrupted; routine gives way to disorganization; and nothing appears to be normal during the crisis. Does anything help? Andrew and Peter found one effective answer when they were confronted with this situation, and that was to bring the Lord into their home at Capernaum. Peter's mother-in-law was sick with a high fever. Her condition must have been a cause for great concern for them to entreat the Lord's help. He responded immediately as Jehovah Ropheka, the Lord who heals, restores. He took hold of the lady's hand and raised her up to full health and strength. And what did she do? She waited on them all, no doubt providing a suitable meal (Mark 1:29-31). Anxiety was changed into joyous fellowship by His presence in the home. Sometimes we need His help in bodily healing; other times we need Him to restore the soul (Psalm 23:3). Jehovah Ropheka can accomplish both for us.

Jehovah Shalom

The arrival of death, that unwelcome visitor, had a shattering effect on the tightly-knit family at Bethany. Sickness overcame Lazarus, and when he died quiet Mary retreated into seclusion with her grief; Martha the practical went to meet the Lord to seek His comfort and help. How wonderfully the picture changes when Lazarus is raised by the spoken word of the Resurrection and the Life! Death vanquished; grief put to flight; the family reunited; and peace reigning. John paints for us a beautiful word picture of the calm setting of the Bethany home at the time of the great reunion (John 12). Jehovah Shalom, the Lord our Peace, is the centre of the tranquillity which prevails.

Contentedly, Lazarus occupies his recognized place at the table, sitting, no doubt, where he can silently adore the One who made the great occasion possible. Mary quietly takes her flask of fragrant oil and pours it upon the feet of Jesus. As the odour fills the house she delicately wipes His feet with the long tresses of her hair. Busy Martha has kept the table supplied in her dedicated way. An attractive picture is presented here of the ideal Christian life with the Lord in the midst: the contentment of Lazarus, the adoration and worship of Mary, and the service of joy of Martha. Not to be overlooked is the changed scene in the home from grief and sorrow to happy fellowship because Jehovah Shalom is the centre of the family circle. When given His rightful place the Lord shows His power to change circumstances; tears to joy, distress to peace.

TWELVE: JEHOVAH NISSI

A paradox in the Christian's life is the possibility of sorrow in times of joy, doubt when assurance is evident, or defeat when victory is assured. We are complex individuals, yet no different from the early disciples. Although the Lord told them He would die and rise again, and they later remembered His words (Luke 24:8), the women were perplexed by the empty tomb (v.4), the apostles treated the report as idle talk (v.11), Peter went home bewildered, amazed (v.12).

The two journeying to Emmaus were discouraged, dismayed, and despairing. They walked and talked as though in a state of shock. It was only the arrival of Jesus as their Companion in the way that enabled them to get things into their true perspective. Here is a lovely word that should comfort us at all times on life's journey: "... Jesus Himself drew near, and went with them" (v.15). Enjoy the truth of the words, but enjoy the spiritual experience even more. His Presence not only reassured the heavy-hearted pair, but their very beings glowed with the warmth of the enlightenment which His opening of the Scriptures brought to them.

Oh, how they constrained, pressured, entreated Him to remain with them! Was their extreme persuasion shown by each one taking an arm to guide Him determinedly into the home? And there the Guest became the Host. As He dined with them, as He took the bread, blessed, and broke it, they would see the unmistakable wound prints in His hands. The Lord was indeed risen! The flag no longer needed to fly at half-mast; it must be run up to the top of the pole again to fly victoriously in the breeze. The King was not just in a humble home with two people, but He was in His banqueting house with beloved ones, and His banner of love was flying victoriously overhead (Song of Songs 2:4). Jehovah Nissi, the Lord is our Banner! This is how we need to know Him. Our times of despair, defeat, and discouragement may continue, but Jehovah Nissi never changes. He is ever victorious. Praise His Name!

THIRTEEN: I AM COMING, LORD!

"In Your presence is fulness of joy; at Your right hand are pleasures for evermore" (Psalm 16:11). She lived in a generation which did not enjoy the many sophistications we know today. Hard work supplemented faith in God, who was able to supply every need. Poverty and adversity were accepted as twin companions in the walk of life; their presence encouraged a sympathetic willingness to help neighbours in all sorts of circumstances. And this is where "Gran" shone. She was wise in the ways of life and death. She was the neighbourhood midwife at all hours of the night and day when babies decided to be born; she was also called at the time of death. She brought ten children of her own into the world, but the demands of such a busy life did not prevent "Gran" from being hospitable to the many Christians who knocked on her door. And nothing was allowed to hinder her from being at the Remembrance, or the prayer and gospel meetings.

At the age of 80 she survived a major operation; and after 90 it was evident that the end of life's long journey had arrived. The family held a vigil. There were tears but no sorrow; there were regrets but no concern. All knew that "Gran" had been waiting to join the Lord Jesus in the heavenly mansions. This was one of the great realities of her Christian experience. The family saw vivid proof of this when she raised herself up, held out her arms, and cried joyfully, "I am coming Lord". She fell back, face aglow. She had gone home as triumphant in death as she had been in life. In a moment, she had passed from the room of death into the eternal dwellings of life and light.

What a fresh reminder that the Christian has nothing to fear in death! It is not the passing through fearful blackness of darkness, but only through the valley of the shadow. There is no shadow without light, and it is a great comfort to know that the Lord, who is our Light, accompanies us through the valley (Psalm 23:4). For the Christian, there is no fear in death. "Perfect love casts out fear" (1 John 4:18). That perfect love was shown in its fullness at Calvary when the eternal Lover of our souls sacrificed His perfect, spotless, holy life, to make possible the forgiveness of all our sins (2 Corinthians 5:21). He has triumphed over sin, Satan, death, and the grave, and He is now living at God's right hand (1 Peter 3:22). His victory is complete, and our rest and security are in our great Conqueror: "Who shall separate us from the love of Christ? Shall tribulation, or distress, or persecution, or famine, or nakedness, or peril, or sword? Yet in all these things we are more than conquerors through Him who loved us" (Romans 8:35,37).

FOURTEEN: GOING HOME

Death is usually the most unwelcome visitor to our homes, and rarely are we prepared for its grim, ungracious arrival. It caused the Master to weep (John 11:35); Abraham to yearn, "that I may bury my dead out of my sight" (Genesis 23:4); and Bildad to describe it as "the king of terrors" (Job 18:14). Solomon spoke of it as a man going to his eternal home; as the silver cord of life having been loosed; as the golden bowl of our days here having been shattered (Ecclesiastes 12:5-7). Death for the Christian is not defeat but victory. That is why we sorrow not as those who have no hope. When Christians die, this world loses something of great value, and so becomes poorer as the result.

The story is told of the home going of that godly servant Dwight L. Moody. In his final moments before entering eternity he exclaimed, "Heaven opens before me! If this is death it is sweet! There is no valley here. God is calling and I must go". When a relative suggested that he was dreaming, Moody answered, "I have looked within the gates ... this is my triumph ... this is my coronation day". We who belong to Christ can envisage the great happenings which follow the rapture. There may be empty spaces in the family circle, in the neighbourhood, on the job. There will be empty houses, church buildings and graves. The salt of the earth will be gone. As for the redeemed, they will be at home with the Lord.

Our hearts should rejoice in the triumphant welcome given to our Lord and Saviour when He returned to heaven after his glorious resurrection. He is the Firstfruits; He is the pioneer of the pathway to the glory-land, and we are going to traverse that same path which leads through the gates of the eternal dwelling-place. "In Your presence is fulness of joy; at Your right hand are pleasures for evermore" (Psalm 16:11). The valley of weeping will then be over, replaced by eternal joy. The valley of the shadow will be passed and replaced by eternal light. This is what causes the Christian to cry, "Come, Lord Jesus".

FIFTEEN: CLAY POTS

Ordinary earthenware pots took on great importance in ancient days, when they became the repositories for gold and silver coins, valuable legal documents, and precious parchments. Those were days when there were no bank vaults or safety deposit boxes, so wealthy potentates used earthen vessels for storing their precious coins and other priceless possessions. Jeremiah tells of keeping in an earthen vessel the deeds to a piece of land which he had purchased (Jeremiah 32:14). It is now many years since the world heard the exciting story of a Middle East shepherd boy throwing into a cave a stone which cracked an earthenware pot, leading to the discovery of the famed Dead Sea scrolls. Ordinary clay pots, made on an uncomplicated potter's wheel, have been used for centuries as storage containers for things of value.

It is encouraging to translate the thought to our spiritual lives, and to see ourselves esteemed by God as earthen pitchers, as were the precious sons of Zion (Lamentations 4:2); or viewed as vessels of mercy (Romans 9:23); of honour (2 Timothy 2:20) or for holding treasure (2 Corinthians 4:7). It is good for us to remember the prayer of Job, "Remember, I pray, that you have made me like clay" (10:9). And the cry of Isaiah, "But now, O Lord, you are our Father; we are the clay, and You our potter; and all we are the work of your hand" (Isaiah 64:8). Then to visit the potter's house and see the once marred vessel made over again into something of usefulness, as the Lord has done with each of us (Jeremiah 18).

The skillful, unerring hands of the Almighty have shaped us for His purpose; to be vessels of trust, responsibility, dependability and honour in His house. This is when we are humbled by His matchless grace, and freely acknowledge that "... we are His workmanship, created in Christ Jesus for good works, which God prepared beforehand that we should walk in them" (Ephesians 2:10). The Greek word 'skeuos' contains the thought of a weak or fragile vessel. Paul uses it to describe the saints as earthen vessels, holding the divine treasure of "the light of the knowledge of the glory of God" (2 Corinthians 4:6,7). Fragile vessels we are at best, but there can be great spiritual joy in store for us if we are willing that His light might shine out to others (Judges 7:20). What kind of vessel do I want to be?

SIXTEEN: THE SAME WITH A DIFFERENCE

Although the Greek word is the same for the "guest-chamber" at Jerusalem, where the Breaking of the Bread was instituted, and the 'inn" at Bethlehem, where Mary and Joseph sought residence, the reception was certainly different. There was a welcome for the Master and His twelve disciples at the one; but there was refusal for Joseph, Mary and the expected Child, at the other.

There was a large upper room fully furnished at the house of welcome in Jerusalem, and the disciples were able to make ready those things which were to speak of His death. "And they ... found as He had said ... and they made ready" (Luke 22:13). But there was no room at the inn, no guest-chamber, and the family chosen to introduce to the world the Son of God from heaven, were relegated to a cattle shed. "And she brought forth her firstborn Son; and wrapped Him in swaddling clothes, and laid Him in a manger, because there was no room for them in the inn" (Luke 2:7). It was in such a place that Mary had to make ready for His birth.

What a contrast with the place where the disciples made ready with those things relating to His death! The Babe was seen by the shepherds lying in the very crib where the fodder was put to feed the animals. What must their thoughts have been at such a sight? What place was this for a Saviour, an anointed Lord? Their reassurance was in the angelic message: "And this will be sign to you, you will find a Babe wrapped in swaddling clothes, lying in a manger" (Luke 2:12).

The two contrasting events seem to reflect human thinking to this day. Some have a place for Him, and some have not. "But as many as received (or welcomed) Him, to them He gave the right to become children of God" (John 1:12). For such He has provided an eternal 'guest chamber' in the heavenly mansions (John 14:2); but until its occupancy is realized, He desires to take up residence in their redeemed hearts. This is the precious thought of comfort conveyed by Paul to early Christians: "that Christ may dwell in your hearts through faith; that you, being rooted and grounded in love, may be able to comprehend" (Ephesians 3:17,18). To dwell means to 'inhabit, reside, settle down'. This is the welcome He wants from, us personally. Are we fully conscious of this? Or are we missing one of the great blessings of our Christian life?

SEVENTEEN: A WIDOW'S FAITH

There was no widow's pension in the days of Elijah. Nevertheless, the widow of Zarephath received a generous guarantee from God because she made the prophet a meal from her tiny store of food. God undertook to provide her with daily food during famine and drought. The God of heaven, who is Jehovah Jireh, the Lord who provides, has not changed since the days of Elijah, and His promises are just as valid now as they were then. Many of God's people can testify to this.

It is from the Lord Jesus that we learn that there were many widows in Israel during the famine of Elijah's day; but it was to the widow of Zarephath that the prophet was sent (Luke 4:26). Human reasoning would count this strange. No husband, a dependent son; where could she obtain food during such a dearth? Elijah had nothing; the widow had little more. Both trusted in Jehovah Jireh. Elijah's request to the widow appears insignificant. A little water, a morsel of bread. But during a famine and drought this would present problems to a faithless, self-protecting person. The widow had a handful of meal, a little oil, a few sticks of wood. Elijah asked her to make his first, and bring it to him, then to get hers and her son's. This was the challenge to faith. But with it always comes the promise. Note the message that Elijah delivered from the LORD, the God of Israel, "The bin of flour shall not be used up, nor shall the jar of oil run dry, until the day the LORD sends rain ..." (1 Kings 17:14).

The Master tells us that the heaven was shut up for three and a half years (Luke 4:25). James tells us that Elijah prayed fervently that it might not rain for three and a half years (5:17). Yet the guarantee was given that the barrel of meal and the cruse of oil would not fail until the day the Lord sent rain on the earth. We can only marvel at the faith of Elijah, and the faith of the widow; but we can draw strength for our day from the same God who is so unfailing in His provision. Paul transmits to us his implicit faith with these words, "And my God shall supply all your need according to His riches in glory by Christ Jesus" (Philippians 4:19). Do you believe this? 'I believe, help my unbelief' (Mark 9:23).

EIGHTEEN: A LESSON FROM THE PAST

What do the next twelve months hold for us as Christians? What are we purposing to do for Him? More quiet times with our Bibles? More use of our talents in His work? More opportunities for testifying? More time for prayer? Prayer to the Christian is one of the essentials for spiritual survival.

Elijah was a man of like nature with us, and he prayed fervently. “And he prayed again” (James 5:17,18). What cries, what pleadings, came from the lips of the holy prophet at mount Carmel, as he asked God to send showers of rain! Picture the scene of the waiting prophet, the watching servant, and the Mighty God etching in His sky the distant cloud as small as a man’s hand. This was His token of prayer answered; the showers of blessing followed (1 Kings 18:42-46). “And he prayed”.

Prosperity has deprived us of equalling the simple living quarters of Elisha. But we are not deprived of the privilege of doing what Elisha did; making them a place of prayer. This is where he brought the boy; and closing the door he prayed to the Lord. He gave his whole being to this challenging situation by stretching himself out upon the lad until their mouths, eyes, and hands met. God answered by restoring the boy to life (2 Kings 4:10). Every family needs its prayer room; a place where we can close the door, give ourselves wholly to the situation of concern, and speak to God about it in the confidence of faith, despite our sorrow of heart. Prayer will demand a price from us. Did the disciples realize this when they asked the Lord, “Teach us to pray, even as John also taught his disciples” (Luke 11:1)? John’s disciples fasted often (Luke 5:33). Fasting is self-denial, and they deprived themselves physically in order to learn to pray, and so benefit spiritually.

Many a treasured project, or planned arrangement, might have to be sacrificed for the needed time of prayer. Whatever the cost, whatever the sacrifice, full repayment will come from the One who loves to answer prayer. "I have heard your prayer, I have seen your tears; surely I will heal you", was God's answer to Hezekiah (2 Kings 20:5). There will be many tears in the year ahead, perhaps more than last year. But the One who put the tears of praying David into His bottle (Psalm 56:8), has our prayers in His golden bowls (Revelation 5:8). This is how much He values our prayers. What of you and me?

NINETEEN: A PENTECOSTAL BLESSING

A Pentecostal blessing - it was given by God on the first Lord's day of this age of grace. We do not here refer to the gift of tongues or to baptism in the Holy Spirit which occurred on that day, but to the divine plan outlined by Peter under the guidance of the newly-given Holy Spirit. It is a blessing which all Christians should accept without question; it is a plan for all Christians to adopt.

The Lord Jesus was raised from the dead on the first day of the week. Fifty days later the Holy Spirit was to descend from heaven, and this He did on a Lord's day, the day of Pentecost. This was the day a multitude heard a restored, divinely energized Peter proclaim the message to which over 3,000 souls responded. Drawing on Old Testament quotations from Joel and David, he appealed with ringing tones, to "Men of Judea, and all who dwell in Jerusalem" (Acts 2:14) to recognize the momentous truth that God's approved Man, Jesus of Nazareth, had conquered death and the grave, and was now glorified in heaven (Acts 2:23,24,34). Then came the great challenge. "Therefore let all the house of Israel know assuredly that God has made this Jesus, whom you crucified, both Lord and Christ" (v.36).

What a culmination to a power-filled message! What an example to preachers of the word today! There are no limitations or restrictions to this message. Peter proclaims clearly and unequivocally that Jesus is Saviour, Lord and King. The Man of the Cross (Jesus), is also the King of the Throne (Christ), and Master Supreme (Lord). There was no partial acceptance on the part of those who heard. They did not claim the forgiveness of sins through faith in Jesus, and then go on their way to follow their own plan. But these redeemed hearts felt the full impact of the Spirit's message through Peter, and they received it with its full consequences that Jesus was to become their Lord: "They then that received his word were baptized" (Acts 2:41). About 3,000 people did this.

What is involved in the word "received"? It means that they welcomed, approved, accepted, and took fully, the truth contained in Peter's words that Jesus was Lord and Christ. No wonder there was such a mighty response on the part of these redeemed, obedient souls to be baptized. And the same willingness was manifested in their embracing and implementing the rest of the divine plan in their individual and collective lives.

This, then, is the plan:

(1) They that received his word

(2) were baptized:

(3) and there were added about 3,000 souls,

(4) and they continued steadfastly in the apostles' teaching,

(5) and fellowship,

(6) in the breaking of bread,

(7) and the prayers (Acts 2:41,42).

These were the seven foundation stones connected with the first church of God of this era. There are no excuses to be found here for not being baptized in water; for not being associated with the divine dwelling place; or for not remembering the Lord as He requested. In their first love, these early disciples were determined to have and to enjoy this Pentecostal blessing. So they were found to be experiencing gladness, praising God (Acts 2:46,47); they were of one heart and soul (Acts 5:32); the word of God increased, and the number of the disciples multiplied (Acts 6:7); and the outcome was peace, edification, and walking in the fear of the Lord (Acts 9:31).

It is one thing to share a common salvation (Jude v.3), which all in the Body of Christ do and can enjoy. But it is quite another thing to comply with the divine plan outlined by Peter on the day of Pentecost. How do these truths affect us? Are we prepared to follow the seven principles laid down in Acts 2:41,42, and thus share in the Pentecostal blessing?

TWENTY: SHATTERED LIVES

A large pane of glass intended for a window had fallen and shattered into thousands of splinters. One moment it was a thing of usefulness, and the next it was being swept up and dumped as useless. Human lives become shattered by sin just as easily and quickly; but we must never underestimate the Lord's ability to renew those lives. Christians sometimes have a tendency to regard their failing fellows as hopeless, but it is not so with the Lord.

A most encouraging illustration is given by Isaiah for us as well as for Israel in the earthly days of Messiah. "A bruised reed He will not break, and the smoking flax He will not quench" (Isaiah 42:1-3). Many who fit into these two categories would have met the Lord Jesus in Palestine, but He did not consign them to the scrap heap. He was in their midst as Jehovah Ropheka, the Lord who restores. David rejoiced in this when he wrote in his shepherd psalm, "He restores my soul" (Psalm 23:3).

The word "bruised" indicates a fragile reed, one which cracks into pieces. Isn't this what happened to Peter in his denial of the Lord Jesus? And it may be so with us too. "I just fell to pieces" is an oft-quoted confession. We thank God that Peter was restored to strengthen his brethren; and the same has been true with us so that we can be used to restore others. When did I last pray for, or seek out, my brother or sister who had been overtaken in a sin (see Galatians 6:1)? Incidentally, the reed was often made into a pen for writing, or a flute for music. When it became worn or cracked it was thrown away and replaced by another. No attempt was made to restore it. But God's ways are not man's ways, and the divine Restorer is able to make a failing Christian a useful, happy instrument again. Onesimus and John Mark are two who were restored and learned to "burn again" for Him and the testimony.

The prodigal son is still the classic example of man's extremity and God's opportunity. One of Britain's greatest preachers was the worst of reprobates before his conversion. A life of crime, which included gambling and pick pocketing, brought on such remorse that he planned suicide. In the passageway of a rooming-house he was about to kill himself with a revolver when he heard a voice reading in an adjoining room the story of the prodigal son from the Bible. The Spirit used this to prevent the suicide and to bring him to Christ. The former pickpocket, who wore gloves for several years after his conversion to remind him of his once evil practice, was used mightily of the Lord to lead others to the Saviour on both sides of the Atlantic.

The principles of repentance and forgiveness seen in the story of the prodigal son may also be applied to wayward children of God. They may regard themselves as shattered glass, smoking flax, or bruised reeds, but scriptural example forbids us to despair concerning them. We must be strengthened by the patience, the expectancy, the forgiveness, and the love of the father in the Lord's parable, and continue to pray steadfastly for them. We must not sin by ceasing to pray for them; we have a responsibility to plead that they will come to themselves, confess their sin, and ask for forgiveness and restoration.

Such was the case with a recent acquaintance of mine. Raised in a Christian home, he was saved, taught in Sunday school, and later youth classes. He was happy in Christian service until one drink of alcohol started him down the slippery slope away from God, home, and friends. "I loved the taste of alcohol" he told me, and the tears appeared as he unfolded his pathetic story. He lost family jobs, and respectability, but he never lost the assurance that his Christian mother would continue to pray for him. Thank God for patient, persistent, praying mothers! The day the wayward son was called to the bedside of his dying father he reinforced himself with alcohol to face the ordeal. Too weak to speak, the father pointed to the son and then to heaven. "I knew what he meant", was the comment. Following 8 years of excessive drinking, and 2 years of sobriety after turning to the Lord in repentance, this "prodigal" has returned home. He is alert to the cause of his downfall.

Christians cannot play fast and loose with alcohol any more than with heroin or marijuana. Is there not a solemn warning to us all in the experience of Nadab and Abihu? The warning given to their father Aaron, high priest in Israel, seems to indicate that they were under the influence of alcohol when they offered strange fire (see Leviticus 10:1-11). Their actions brought shame on their family and their nation. "Therefore let him that thinks he stands take heed lest he fall" (1 Corinthians 10:12).

TWENTY-ONE: JUMPING TO CONCLUSIONS

"Startling" is one way to describe a scriptural incident in which some of Israel's tribes almost went to war with each other because of a sad case of misunderstanding. Wrong decisions and bad judgements, with their resultant grief and sorrow, are often the outcome of assumptions and jumping to conclusions. These two barriers to good communication have always been with us. Obviously, God's people are not exempt from them.

After Joshua's triumphs, the land of Canaan became the inheritance of Israel. The tribes were allocated their territories, and Reuben, Gad, and the half-tribe of Manasseh were given their possession in Gilead, on the other side of the River Jordan. Before they left Shiloh to possess their land, Joshua commended them for keeping the commandments of the Lord. Sending them on their journey with great wealth of gold, silver, and cattle, and a blessing, Joshua encouraged them to "... take careful heed to do the commandment and the law which Moses the servant of the Lord commanded you, to love the Lord your God, to walk in all His ways, to keep His commandments, to hold fast to Him, and to serve Him with all your heart and with all your soul" (Joshua 22:5,6).

The spirit among all the tribes seemed to be exceedingly good at this time, but it was not long before a rift looked like developing because someone had jumped to a wrong conclusion. A rumour was started, and the resulting consequences were almost disastrous. Observe carefully the following words recorded by the Spirit: "And the children of Israel heard someone say ..." (Joshua 22:11). What had they heard? That the two and a half tribes had built an altar "in the region of the Jordan - on the children of Israel's side".

Without apparent further enquiry, "the whole congregation of the children of Israel gathered together at Shiloh to go to war against them" (v.12). What a frightening decision! Made, no doubt, with the best intentions in the world of guarding God's honour. But how contrary to the instruction given by Moses to the nation! He had incorporated in Israel's constitution the wise advice that: "If you hear someone in one of your cities, which the Lord your God gives you to dwell in, saying, 'Corrupt men have gone out from among you and enticed the inhabitants of their city, saying, "Let us go and serve other gods"'—which you have not known - then you shall inquire, search out, and ask diligently (Deuteronomy 13:12-14). Then comes the qualification before action is taken: "And if it is indeed true and certain that such an abomination was committed among you, you shall surely strike the inhabitants of that city with the edge of the sword, utterly destroying it, all that is in it and its livestock - with the edge of the sword" (vv.14,15). Not until the truth was known, after search and diligent enquiry, was a conclusion to be reached. Decisions cannot be reached on unconfirmed stories. Einstein said on one occasion: "Never determine anything as a matter of opinion that can be determined as a matter of fact".

Led by Phinehas, the son of Eleazar the priest, ten princes of Israel confronted the tribes of Reuben, Gad, and Manasseh, and alleged "What treachery is this that you have committed against the God of Israel ... in that you have built for yourselves an altar, that you might rebel this day against the Lord?" (Joshua 22:16). To charges of trespass and rebellion were added those of iniquity like Peor, and turning away from following the LORD (vv.18,19). What a sad situation had now developed! How explosive it had all become! We cannot but admire the gracious response from those who were accused. No hostility, just a straightforward, truthful answer.

The Lord knew, they said, that they had not built the altar out of trespass or rebellion, or to offer sacrifices; but as a safeguard for their children. "but that it may be a witness between you and us ... that your descendants may not say to our descendants in time to come, 'You have no part in the Lord.' ...far be it from us that we should rebel against the Lord" (vv.27-29). Their explanation, with its additional assurance that the only altar for sacrifice and service they acknowledged was the one before His tabernacle, was accepted by Phinehas and the princes, and in turn by Israel (v.33). And so was avoided unnecessary bloodshed, which otherwise might have torn Israel apart for generations.

It might be said that the two and a half tribes were wrong in building the altar without consulting the other tribes. On the other hand, it seems quite clear that the tribes with the majority had over-reacted; instead of thoughts of war and instead of an emotional pre-judgement, they would have done better to follow out peacefully the wisdom of Moses in carrying out quiet, diligent search and enquiry.

How true that, "whatever things were written before were written for our learning, that we through the patience and comfort of the Scriptures might have hope" (Romans 15:4). Perhaps there is a lesson for us to learn from Israel's experience, that we might be sure before we act. Then the scripture will be fulfilled that "wisdom is justified of all her children" (Luke 7:35).

TWENTY-TWO: DUTCH ELM DISEASE AND THE CHRISTIAN

Dutch elm disease has spread across Europe, jumped the Channel to England, and is now being found 6,000 miles away in Canada and the USA. A beetle, one of the smallest of God's creatures, is held responsible for the fatal infection. Nothing, so far, seems able to hinder its deadly work. Thousands of trees have already died, and thousands more are doomed. The elm is being destroyed by a fungus which cuts off the water supply to the leaf, and the massive, green-leafed, healthy elm tree withers and dies. It must then be uprooted as a precautionary measure. The name, Dutch elm disease, is somewhat misleading. The tree is not a Dutch elm, but the link is brought about through the discovery decades ago in Holland of the fungus responsible for the death of the elm. It is not always possible to diagnose the disease until the fatal damage has occurred, and because a tree cannot cry for help, the outward symptoms are the only indicators of imminent death.

Trees play such an important part in God's dealings with man, and the fact that He speaks of us individually as trees (Psalm 1:3), and desires us to be green-leafed and fruitful, causes us to consider the tragedy of the elm as a parable with spiritual significance to Christians. Israel were forbidden to destroy trees when they besieged a city (Deuteronomy 20:19 KJV). It appears as if God sees us in a church of God collectively as a miniature garden of Eden. Paul told the Corinthians that they were God's husbandry (1 Corinthians 3:9). They were His tilled land, a productive garden, a place of delights, an enclosed area. We are

His husbandry, and the Lord Jesus confirms that His Father is the Husbandman (John 15:1).

In Eden, Adam was the husbandman, and God loved to walk and talk with him amidst the beauty and the fragrance of the place He gave Adam to keep. It was a place fenced off from the field, and God must have grieved when "the serpent ... the beast of the field" (Genesis 3:1) entered the husbandry of God. Satan must be kept out or he will wreak havoc in churches of God today. From the beginning, the Lord intended that blessing should be derived from trees, and the following descriptions might help us to see what should characterize us as trees planted by the rivers of water. The vine is associated with the wine of joy, and the fig with satisfying fruit; the cedar is a wood of great usefulness and most pleasant fragrance; the oak indicates strength, while the apple and the pomegranate provide pleasant, refreshing fruit; and the olive produces fresh oil for a healthy countenance. There are also trees for rest (Genesis 18:4), and for sweetness (Exodus 15:25).

From these illustrations, we can see the worth of what we have to protect, and because of this the enemy will be using things little and great to ruin with the blight, mildew, and fungus of sin and temptation our lives as trees for God. Let us make it our aim to be "trees of the LORD ... full of sap" (Psalm 104:16 KJV) and 'like a green olive tree in the house of God" (Psalm 52:8).

TWENTY-THREE: HOW MOTHERS PRAY

It has been said that the hand which rocks the cradle rules the world. Of the truth of this we are unsure, but we are certain that greater things have been wrought by a mother's prayer than this world realizes. John Newton, author of "Amazing Grace", lost his mother, the one clear guiding-star of his early life, at the age of seven. But up to that time she prayed with him, and for him, every day. Faithfully she sowed the good seed of the word of God in the fertile soil of this young life, and she grieved on her deathbed at leaving him to the mercy of a rough world.

He wrote later: "In evil long I took delight, unawed by shame or fear"; and sin brought him to the lowest depths of degradation. He became the slave of a slave woman, and he fed on the crusts of bread which she threw to him under the table. During a terrible storm when the ship in which he served threatened to capsize, Newton began to pray. His mother's example and godly instruction were bearing fruit in strange circumstances. He cried for mercy, and "the Lord came from on high and delivered me out of deep waters", he was to write later. He was certainly the most suitable person to pen the memorable words of the hymn, "Amazing grace how sweet the sound, Which saved a wretch like me".

But for the prayers of Hannah, one of Scripture's great women of faith, and the spectacular answer she received, it is questionable if her husband, Elkanah, would ever have found mention in the divine record. Dispirited, heartbroken, tormented, this godly soul shed copious tears, but she did not relax her faith in God. Although afflicted by an inability to have children, she prayed, and prayed, and prayed for a son. "Is anything too hard for the LORD?" (Genesis 18:14). "With God all things are possible" (Matthew 19:26). These two scriptures seem so suited to her case. She held on to the invisible cord of faith which joined her to the throne of heaven. Do you sometimes ask, as the disciples once asked, "Lord, teach us to pray"? Listen in to Hannah, and learn a precious lesson. "O LORD ... look on the affliction of your maidservant ... remember me, and not forget ... but will give your maidservant a male child ..." (1 Samuel 1:11). Look! Remember! Give!

These were pleadings of faith, and it is then written: "She continued praying before the LORD: ... she spoke in her heart; only her lips moved ... I ... poured out my soul before the LORD" (vv. 12-15). There was no giving up with this dear woman until her prayer was answered, and her hope realized. Then follow these revivifying words: "and the LORD remembered her" (v.19). Encouraging words, too, for all who plead at the eternal throne.

Wonderful is the change in the soul which receives an answer to prayer. This was true of Hannah, whose name means, gracious, merciful, restful. God gave her a son, the longing of her heart, and she called his name Samuel ("heard, or asked of God"). How long Hannah prayed we don't know; but the delay in God's answer, and the resulting reproach from others, did not cause her to faint in her soul. Notice her words to aged Eli: "I am the woman that stood by you here, praying to the LORD. For this child I prayed; and the LORD has granted me my petition" (vv.26,27). Standing and praying, seem to typify Hannah. This shows a determination, a patience, an expectancy of faith. And having received her answer, this praying woman became a worshipping woman (v.28, Revised Version margin).

We should not underestimate the prayer of a mother for her son, or for a son. Mrs Newton's prayer life had its influence on son John who, in turn, by his Christian life greatly influenced such men as Cowper, Wilberforce, and Buchanan. The last named evangelized the East Indies and wrote a book which moved Judson to visit Burma. And what shall we say of Hannah? Her son became a great prophet like unto Moses. "But a woman that fears the LORD, she shall be praised. Give her of the fruit of her hands; and let her works praise her in the gates."

TWENTY-FOUR: THE SINGING SAINT

Deathbed utterances from some of earth's mighty ones have been recorded for posterity; but they are not to be compared with those of God's heroes and heroines. One of the Lord's best, a true shepherd of the flock, once caused the walls and ceilings of a hospital's ward to ring with his beautiful tenor rendering of "Blessed assurance, Jesus is mine". It caused some consternation, but much admiration. For who could despise a Christian hymning his final doxology to an unarranged hospital congregation, before entering the portals of heaven? One person of authority did object, and in stern tones asked the doctor-friend of the singing saint: "Who is this man that sings such hymns"? Perhaps she was astounded, or secretly touched; an occurrence such as this had not happened in the hospital before. But what a glorious, victorious epitaph! "Blessed are those that dwell in Your house: they will be still praising You. Blessed is the man whose strength is in You" (Psalm 84:4,5).

One of God's treasures, a devout lady who loved her Lord and His precious word, was coming to the end of life's journey in hospital. Drawing near to her bedside, I whispered: "Let not your heart be troubled". Before I could complete the verse she opened her eyes, and said quite firmly: "My heart isn't troubled". She closed them again indicating a finality of peace and contentment; a restful waiting for the Lord to take her home. Her faith in the Saviour was ample provision for the brief journey through the valley of the shadow. "And they that know Your name will put their trust in You; for You LORD, have not forsaken those that seek You" (Psalm 9:10).

Great people deserve great epitaphs. It is said of John Bunyan that he was saved through the Lord's words: "and the one that comes to Me I will by no means cast out" (John 6:37). His last words on earth were: "Take me for I come to Thee". John Knox rested his soul on the verse: "And this is eternal life, that they may know You, the only true God, and Jesus Christ whom You have sent" (John 17:3). "That", said God's mighty, fearless servant, "is where I cast my first anchor". To which we add our Amen!

TWENTY-FIVE: THE FAULTY COMPASS

It was winter. The two hunters were comfortable and warm as they slept overnight in their wilderness cabin in northern British Columbia. The morning revealed a deep blanket of fresh snow, which gave the countryside an entirely different appearance from the night before. Standing in the doorway together they discussed their plans. "This is our direction", remarked the one, indicating with his finger. The other seemed uncertain. "My compass says we should go the opposite way", he answered. Both men were experienced in the ways of the wild, and finally they agreed to follow the compass. For more than an hour the two tramped through the deep snow before realizing that they were not only lost, but had headed in the wrong direction. They had been misled by the compass. An impossibility, some say, because the instrument is so carefully made and tested. But a later check revealed that it did have a defect. Two concerned hunters found their way back to their cabin safely, and as a result of their experience they were, no doubt, much wiser.

God has a compass for Christians. It is His word, the Bible. It will never lead a person astray. It is never wrong. We can trust it completely. We can rest our lives on it for eternity. It is infallible. Sir William Osler, once described as "the greatest physician in history", gave this advice to his medical students: "Begin the day with Christ and His prayer ... Learn to know your Bible ... its touch has still its ancient power..." The Bible is the Voice of God, which alone is able to reach dead souls and give them eternal life. We need to know our Bibles in the personal work of leading people to Christ. We must have confidence in its power over our own lives and the lives of others. The very power God used in creation is contained in every word of Scripture. The worlds were brought into existence by the word of God (Hebrews 11:3). "For He spoke, and it was done; He commanded, and it stood fast" (Psalm 33:9). Think of this other miracle of creation. "And God said, Let there be light: and there was light" (Genesis 1:3). Instantly, light replaced the darkness.

According to records in China, the compass was in use eighteen hundred years ago; to be exact, 121 A.D. One of the first consisted of a magnetized needle floating on a piece of cork in a bowl of water. But sailors who did not have a compass carried birds aboard their ships. Sailors who were lost released the birds and hopefully followed them to land. We are thankful that we are not dependent on this method today. To say the least, it proved to be risky, and certainly inaccurate.

Some Christians, however, use the Bible on a "hit and miss" basis, which is not a method to be imitated. Life is far too serious, it has too many uncertainties, dangers, problems, and temptations. The Bible must be used on a regular, active basis, if we are to get its full benefit. We need something dependable by which to steer accurately our 'craft' (our lives) on the ocean of life. There are rocks to avoid; there are high seas to battle; there are safe harbours to find. We need the Bible as our compass. Let these Scriptures re-assure us of the absolute reliability of God's Book.

The word of the Lord is RIGHT (Psalm 33:4); TRUE (Psalm 119:160); GOOD (Isaiah 39:8); POWERFUL (Luke 4:32); LIVING (Hebrews 4:12); PURE (Proverbs 30:5). Do you have implicit trust in your Bible? Do you give it the value it deserves? It is light in a world of darkness; it is a living thing in a dead world. The word of God is eternal (1 Peter 1:23); it is to be trusted (Psalm 119:42); it should be hidden in our hearts (Psalm

119:11); we should hear its voice (Jeremiah 17:20). John, the apostle of love, lived in days similar to our own. The Bible was under attack and disbelieved and Christians were forsaking the Faith. He left these words perhaps for you: "I have written to you, young men, because you are strong, and the word of God abides in you, and you have overcome the wicked one" (1 John 2:14).

It is important to build ourselves healthy bodies by good food, exercise, and plenty of rest; it is more important to apply these things to our spiritual lives by obeying the voice of our Master who said: "Man shall not live by bread alone, but by every word that proceeds from the mouth of God" (Matthew 4:4).

TWENTY-SIX: WONDERFUL PLACES

Ziklag, where he strengthened himself in the Lord his God (1 Samuel 30:1-6), and Adullam's cave (1 Samuel 22:1,2), were two places David would not forget. The winepress, where he received the assurance "The LORD is with you, you mighty man of valour", was a memorable place for Gideon (Judges 6:12). As for Moses, his never-to-be-forgotten places were the bush, the mountain top, the Tent, and the cleft of the rock. Those who had such great experiences invariably became great for God for they heard the voice of the Eternal, and learned His omnipotent ways. The same wonderful places of meditation, communion, prayer, and protection, are available to the Lord's disciples today if we, too, long for our spiritual lives to be strengthened and blessed.

Moses saw, and heard, and learned things which left on him their indelible impression. They were so necessary in assisting him as the fearless leader of a nation emancipated from Egypt. He was to shepherd the flock of God, a task far more important than tending Jethro's sheep (Exodus 3). Awaiting Moses, too, was the place of the rock. Egypt and the Red Sea were now behind him, and a redeemed people were to build for God a glorious dwelling-place in the desert en route to the Promised Land. While Moses was receiving the plan of the Tabernacle, and the tablets of stone, on Mount Sinai, Aaron was busy down below with the golden calf. God's anger over this almost resulted in Israel's being consumed (Exodus 33:5).

For a time, God was silent with His people, and it was a memorable day when Moses first disappeared into the Tent, followed by the gaze of an anxious people, and the Lord spoke to him "face to face, as a man speaks to his friend" (Exodus 33:11). As at the bush, Moses never forgot that early encounter of the Tent. In the Eternal Presence, he pleaded the promise of grace, and sought the assurance of the continuing Presence of Jehovah. He cried, "... show me ... that I may know You ... that I may find grace ... and consider ... this ... Your people". And the divine answer was, "My presence shall go with you, and I will give you rest" (vv.12-14). The bush, the mountain, the Tent, all unforgettable for Moses. Wonderful places of experience, but there awaited him yet, the place of the rock.

God, you see, is never completely finished in His dealings with His servants, with you and me, on earth. He gives us as much as we can contain, and leaves us longing for more. And so the eyes which saw the bush burn, earnestly desired to see the glory. Did ever a prayer escape the lips of a man like that of pleading Moses on that day? Just as if nothing else mattered, he cried: "Shew me, I pray Thee, Thy glory" (v.18). That prayer was to have a remarkable answer hundreds of years later; and it was to be on a different mountain, and in the Promised Land. Yes, Moses did enter the land, and with Elijah he saw the majesty of Messiah on the holy mount of Transfiguration. He saw His face shining as the sun, and His garments as white as the light (Matthew 17:1-8). Moses could then have said, "We beheld His glory" (John 1:14).

But at the place of the rock he was told, "Thou canst not see My face: for man shall not see Me and live" (v.20). Then came an invitation to an experience which would brand itself on Moses until the day of his death in Moab. "And the LORD said, Behold, there is a place by Me, and thou shalt stand upon the rock; And it shall come to pass, while My glory passeth by, that I will put thee in a cleft of a rock, and will cover thee with My hand until I have passed by" (v.22). Meditate on the wonder of this experience. A place by Me! Standing upon the rock! Hidden in the cleft of the rock! And the mighty hand of God as a cover! Could Moses ever forget? Never! He would live in the strength of what he had heard and seen for many days.

What of us? This, too, is the story of our full salvation, and all that accompanies it; the story of Calvary and all the contingent blessings of His presence, protection, and power. But we must seek the reassurance of the experience as Moses did. We must come to the unforgettable places of prayer, as Moses did, for refreshment of soul, for strength for the day.

"A wonderful Saviour is Jesus my Lord,

A wonderful Saviour to me;

He hideth my soul in the cleft of the rock,

Where rivers of pleasure I see.

He hideth my soul in the cleft of the rock,

That shadows a dry, thirsty land;

He hideth my life in the depth of His love,

And covers me there with His hand."

TWENTY-SEVEN: APOLLOS THE BROTHER

That is how Paul described him - not my fellow-elder, or fellow-worker, or fellow countryman. Not "our beloved brother", as Peter once described Paul (2 Peter 3:15). "But as touching Apollos the brother, I besought him much to come unto you with the brethren" (1 Corinthians 16:12). Was Paul using a term of endearment? Or an expression of commendation? Whatever was in his mind the term "the brother" is elevated to a status of great respect, for Apollos was a man highly regarded in the churches of God. His name means "one who destroys or lays waste", a description which seems to be entirely opposed to the nature of this gifted servant of the Lord (1 Corinthians 3:22). It was more suited to Paul before his conversion, for he was a destroyer, a disrupter, a persecutor of God's workers and works. But Apollos was a builder for the Lord (Acts 18:27,28).

Apollos had been a follower of John the Baptist, and his godly character as a disciple manifested itself when he first came into contact with those two gems of Israel, Priscilla and Aquila, who had dedicated themselves to the Way (Acts 18:1-3; 24-28). Although he is described as a learned or eloquent man, mighty in the Scriptures, instructed in the way of the Lord, and fervent in spirit, he was not resistant to the words of truth which this dear, devotional husband and wife, imparted to him. Humbly and graciously he listened as they "expounded unto him the way of God more carefully" (v.26). This was the great turning point in the life of Apollos, and he went on to be a man of might in the churches of God.

What a loss it would have been to God and His people if Apollos had been proud, arrogant, or non-receptive to the exhortations of Priscilla and Aquila. They heard him speak boldly in the synagogue, and "they took him unto them, and expounded unto him the way of God more carefully". Here are wonderful words of advice on how to communicate the truth. The Spirit has left on record for our help the gracious method of a loving approach to people. "They took him unto them".

Apollos was to labour in Corinth with great power. He was content to follow Paul the planter as Apollos the waterer (1 Corinthians 3:6). And so this good servant of the Lord is commended as "Apollos the brother".

TWENTY-EIGHT: INFLATION

Is inflation a great help or a great danger? When it is used for safety purposes by the increasing of air in life-jackets or vehicle tyres, inflation is an asset. But when it involves the issuing of more money than is justified by the amount of a nation's resources, then economic inflation becomes a dangerous menace! Christians should be happy that there is no inflation in God's economy. The spiritual riches available to us do not, and cannot, depreciate in value. They can only increase. As we check regularly the assets we have in an earthly bank, so we should know what we have in our spiritual bank. Paul, who wrote once of the unsearchable riches of Christ, gives us this list of what is available to us:

> The riches of His goodness; of His forbearance; of His longsuffering (Romans 2:4);
>
> The riches of His glory (Romans 9:23);
>
> The riches of wisdom and knowledge (Romans 11:33);
>
> The riches of liberality (2 Corinthians 8:2);
>
> The riches of His grace (Ephesians 1:7);
>
> The riches of the glory of His inheritance (Ephesians 1:18);
>
> The exceeding riches of His grace (Ephesians 2:7);

> The unsearchable riches of Christ (Ephesians 3:8); and
>
> The riches of the full assurance of understanding (Colossians 2:2).

Can there be such a thing as a poor Christian when such spiritual wealth is there for our possession? We are dealing here with divine goodness, divine wisdom, divine grace, divine understanding. What an enrichment each one is to the divine life which we have received in Christ! Let us, then, reveal our riches to a world which is perplexed by, and discontented with, the diminishing value of corrupt riches (James 5:2). As we manifest divine grace, and goodness, and understanding, so we are giving souls a glimpse of the unsearchable riches of Christ. Dare we forget that we are vessels of mercy upon whom God has bestowed the riches of His glory (Romans 9:23)?

TWENTY-NINE: WOMEN – INFERIOR OR SUBJECT? (PART 1)

Nowhere in Scripture is it suggested that the woman is inferior to the man; nor is she considered to be a person without responsibility. In the kingdom of God, she is viewed as having a definite role. She will be just as answerable as the man at the judgement-seat of Christ as to how she fills that role. We read in the Gospels and the Epistles of ministering women (Luke 8:3); of women who teach (Titus 2:3); and of women who pray and prophesy (1 Corinthians 11:5). Yet, Paul says, "I permit not a woman to teach ... but to be in quietness" (1 Timothy 2:12). Does this suggest a conflict, a contradiction? We shall return to this question next time.

In early churches of God, a number of striking testimonies were paid to women and their work. Priscilla, for example, unquestionably played a large part in leading Apollos into the truth. It is interesting to note that in order to accomplish the work of expounding unto him "the way of God more carefully", Priscilla, and her husband, Aquila, took Apollos into their home (Acts 18:25-26). This seemed typical of the devoted Christian couple, who were to become Paul's fellow-workers. When they lived in Rome he remembered them with affection, and "the church that is in their house" (Romans 16:4,5). Priscilla's part in building up the church of God obviously took place in her home.

Dorcas, like all of God's good women, was known more for what she did than what she said. This tribute to her is recorded for ever: "This woman was full of good works, and almsdeeds which she did" (Acts 9:36-37). The weeping Christians who greeted Peter, showed him the coats and garments which Dorcas had made while she was with them (v.39). Did Dorcas not speak at all? It is hardly likely that she would not tell of the love of the Lord Jesus as Saviour, Master and Lord, as she bestowed her garments on needy souls.

Phoebe, a deaconess of the church in Cenchreae, performed a different service. It is quite possible that she was a wealthy woman, and used her means to provide sustenance for the saints and for others. Her home would be open for Christian hospitality, as in the case of Lydia at Philippi (Acts 16:15). Paul's commendation of Phoebe that she was "a succourer of many", adds substance to these thoughts.

God's esteem for women and their work is revealed in a multitude of ways. The labour and materials for the Tabernacle, God's house in the wilderness, were not all provided by the men. It delights the heart to read: "And all the women that were wise-hearted did spin with their hands, and brought that which they had spun, the blue, and the purple, the scarlet, and the fine linen. And all the women whose heart stirred them up in wisdom spun the goats' hair" (Exodus 35:25,26). Hidden from the eyes of many in the camp of Israel, but observed by the God of heaven, these dear women worked away skillfully in their tents, hour after hour, day after day, spinning the beautiful curtains for the divine dwelling. And they did it wisely! Dare anyone say that their work, done in the home, was any less skillful than that performed, perhaps more publicly, in gold, silver and copper by Bezalel, Oholiab, and their fellows (Exodus 36:1)?

The precious, attractive material, of such glorious, divinely chosen colours handled so skilfully in the tents of Israel's women, speaks of the excellencies of Christ. In their day, Priscilla, Lydia, Dorcas, Phoebe, and a host of other godly women, revealed these very excellencies, and so set a magnificent example for their sisters in churches of God today.

THIRTY: WOMEN – INFERIOR OR SUBJECT? (PART 2)

Let us now answer the question posed last time. We commence with the ministering women who accompanied the Lord Jesus. It is clear from the Scriptures that the Lord Jesus, the twelve being with Him, did the preaching; and the women, we are not told how many, acted as their attending servants, and generally cared for their needs (Luke 8:1-3). Their loving care has been noted for eternity.

The teaching women of Titus 2 were mature Christians in churches of God, who were encouraged to show young wives the value and importance of family life, and the actions and disciplines necessary to a happy Christian home. Love for husband and children would be stressed, and the great value of being workers at home, and the need for subjection to their husbands (Titus 2:1-5). What grace, wisdom and skill would be necessary to accomplish such a task to the glory of God! The women "praying and prophesying" were functioning as part of the church in Corinth and would not be doing anything different from their sisters in churches of God today. When Paul said of the Thessalonians, "From you hath sounded forth the word of the Lord", he was referring to the church in its entirety; the young, the old, the brothers, the sisters, the deacons, the overseers. So it was in Corinth. Not all were doing the public preaching, or the public praying, but the brethren elected by the Spirit to pray and to preach, did soon behalf of the church. They were the voice of the church.

So at a prayer meeting, the brother who leads the assembly prays audibly on behalf of all, so all pray, and all say the Amen. Equally, when a brother ministers publicly, it is on behalf of the church, and his God-given message receives the united support of the saints. He speaks not for himself but for the church, and so all in the church are speaking as one. And this applies too, in judgement and reception of saints. It is the church of God which puts away, and the church of God which receives. Paul makes this evident when writing to put away the wicked man, and later to restore him as a repentant brother (1 Corinthians 5:13; 2 Corinthians 2:5-8). These instructions were given to the church of God in Corinth. In any public notification overseers act on behalf of the church.

When Paul writes to the same Corinthian Christians about the sisters wearing the veil as a head covering (1 Corinthians 11), he is emphasizing authority and subjection. He instructs the woman to cover her head when the assembly meets to preach, to teach, to pray, and to worship. In so doing she acknowledges the headship of the man, who in turn has his head uncovered, and is subject to the Headship of Christ. The truth of subjection is also brought out in the apostolic injunction that the woman was not permitted to teach publicly in the church of God, nor to have dominion over the man, but she was to be in quietness (1 Timothy 2:8-12).

These divine restrictions, however, did not exclude the sister from all service, as we have seen in the lives of others. There is much for a woman to do, and good examples are left for her in Priscilla, Dorcas, Lydia, Phoebe; the mature women under Titus' jurisdiction, and the serving women of Paul's day. It is a great joy to God to see brethren bearing the burdens He intends for them; and for sisters to fill joyfully the role He has purposed for them.

The united labours of both will contribute to a healthy, virile church of God.

THIRTY-ONE: FATHER, FORGIVE THEM

"Father, forgive them" (Luke 23:34)

Death by crucifixion was first conceived by the Phoenicians, and copied by Rome. Stoning was Israel's punishment; yet the piercing of the hands and feet of the Lord was a fulfilment of prophecy (Psalm 22:16; John 19:37). The wooden cross, or stake, was laid on the ground, and the soldiers wrestled the victim into a prostrate position on it. His hands and feet were held forcibly in place as the spikes were ruthlessly driven into the flesh, binding the victim to the wood.

"And it was the third hour and they crucified Him" (Mark 15:25). How amazed the soldiers must have been by the gentle, willing, and completely unresisting attitude of the Lord Jesus! No reviling, only a heart-rending, prayerful cry, "Father, forgive them; for they know not what they do". What a marked contrast He is to all others! How He stands out so nobly, so majestically! And His cry was of forgiveness! Was it for His executioners? Or was the plea to heaven's Throne for His own people? Or was it a universal prayer of forgiveness? The Lord predicted that the Jews would deliver Him to the Gentiles for crucifixion (Matthew 20:19); and the early disciples distinguished between "Herod and Pontius Pilate, with the Gentiles and peoples of Israel", being gathered together against the Lord Jesus. It was all part of the prophetic fulfilment in its embracing of the Gentiles and the kings of the earth (Acts 4:25-28). None then need be exempt from the Saviour's plea for forgiveness. The living words contain the divine power for saving any man's soul.

"We were not with the faithful few

Who stood Thy bitter cross around,

Nor heard Thy prayer for those who slew,

Nor felt the earthquake rock the ground.

We saw no spear-wound pierce Thy side;

Yet we believe that Thou hast died."

(H. J. Buckoll)

"Today shalt thou be with Me in Paradise" (Luke 23:43)

Callous indifference; cruel mocking; scoffing and taunting, all contributed to the tense atmosphere which built up around the Cross whilst, untouched by the excruciating pain endured by the crucified, the Jewish rulers vented their spleen on the Lord Jesus. "He saved others: let Him save Himself, if this is the Christ of God, His Chosen", they shouted. The soldiers joined them taunting, "If Thou art the King of the Jews, save Thyself" (Luke 23:37). The two robbers added their chorus of reproaches, but the Lord quietly suffered it all (Matthew 27:44). Then followed a dialogue between the two thieves which resulted in one condemning and the other defending the Saviour. "This Man", the one exclaimed, "hath done nothing amiss". What an awakening! What a discovery! It led to his salvation. He realized that the Man in the midst was the King. With newly found faith he cried, "Jesus, remember me when Thou comest in Thy kingdom". Instantly came the reply of total forgiveness and eternal hope, "Today shalt thou be with Me in Paradise" (Luke 23:39-43). Only the Eternal One could make such a promise and fulfil it.

THIRTY-TWO: BEHOLD THY SON

"Woman, behold, thy son! Behold, thy mother!" (John 19:26,27)

A strange assortment of humanity was drawn, as by a magnet, to that "Green hill ... outside the city wall". Those who enjoy the gruesome joined those who scorned; and those who were intrigued by the spectacular end to the gentle Man who performed miracles, and who spoke kindly words, might have stood sympathetically with those who loved the One on the middle cross. The location of Peter is not recorded. There were some disciples who stood afar off. Is it the fear of identification with Him which causes this, or the physical inability to cope with the close-up view of a loved One enduring prolonged grief and pain? Neither deterred the faithful women, who held silent, loving vigil with John, so close to the suffering Saviour. John records: "But there were standing by the Cross of Jesus His mother, and His mother's sister, Mary the wife of Clopas, and Mary Magdalene. When Jesus therefore saw His mother, and the disciple standing by, whom He loved, He saith unto His mother, Woman, behold, thy Son! Then saith He to the disciple, Behold, thy mother! And from that hour the disciple took her unto his own home" (John 19:25-27).

Mary had been chosen by God from among all women to give birth to the Christ-child. Her eyes must have filled with tears of joy when she first nestled the Babe in her arms. She had been highly honoured by heaven in the care, the feeding of, and in providing for, the young Child, the Youth and the growing Man. And now in His closing hours she beholds Him hanging on the accursed Cross. No tears of joy in this scene, but many of grief and sorrow. How the deep emotions of a mother's love must have flooded her soul as she looked on His suffering body and pain-wracked yet gracious face. The moment had also now come for her delicate soul to receive the piercing of the sword foretold at His birth, "that thoughts out of many hearts may be revealed" (Luke 2:35). It took the Cross, and words from the Saviour Himself, to reveal to Mary her part in the great divine plan enacted by Him to bring eternal blessing to the human race. He who in early life was sheltered by this dear woman, now makes provision for her before He dies. It was the second of His final bequests. The first was a place in Paradise for the dying thief; and now He committed Mary into the care of John, the beloved, who took her to his home.

THIRTY-THREE: WHY HAVE YOU FORSAKEN ME?

"My God, My God, why hast Thou forsaken Me?" (Matthew 27:46)

Three hours of excruciating torture have been endured without complaint by God's dear Son. In the light of such intense suffering our redeemed hearts are forced to enquire: "I wonder what He saw in me to suffer such deep agony?" Mercilessly the sun's rays have beaten down on His defenceless head, intensifying His sufferings; then, mercifully, the sun was obscured and darkness descended upon the whole land. Can we not see through the eyes of faith that He must know this darkness that we might be saved from the blackness of darkness forever? He must sink in deep mire, where sin has taken us, that we might know beneath us the strength of the Everlasting Arms. He must know the waves and billows of God's wrath, that we might escape the storm. He must know the fire of God's judgement, that we might be saved from the fires of hell. The blackness, the fury, the fire, were all our due, but He, as our sin-Bearer, endured it all. We deserved to be forsaken by a holy God because of sin, but He willingly took our place.

Mystery of mysteries, that God should forsake His Son! If the burning bush was holy ground for Moses, how much more Calvary to the redeemed heart. Holy ground, burnt ground; for where He was consumed in our place by the fires of God's wrath, we stand protected, knowing that the fire cannot touch that place again.

"'Neath Thy cross I stand and worship,

Suffering Man, yet conquering God!

Resting on Thy death-atonement,

Weary, I lay down my load."

"I thirst" (John 19:28)

Out of the prevailing darkness came the Lord's cry, "I thirst". Yet another of the prophetic utterances must be fulfilled. "My strength is dried up like a potsherd; and My tongue cleaveth to My jaws" (Psalm 22:15). "I am weary with My crying; My throat is dried" (Psalm 69:3). "And in My thirst they gave Me vinegar to drink" (Psalm 69:21). The One who cried to a thirsty nation, "Come unto Me, and drink" (John 7:37), Himself knew extreme thirst on the Cross. The One who gave to a needy, sinful woman the water of life, was Himself forced to cry, "I thirst". When He sat at Sychar's well He was weary with His journey and asked the Samaritan woman, "Give Me to drink". "The well is deep" said the Samaritan woman when the Lord spoke of the living water which He would give; but it was not so deep as the well of His suffering on the Cross.

It is about the ninth hour of the crucifixion day when His desperate cry is heard. The end of the battle of all battles is now in sight and the divine Warrior, the Captain of our salvation, longs for a thirst-quenching drink of cool water. The response to His cry of "I thirst" appeared to be immediate; but the callous nature with which man had been imbued by sin, revealed itself in a sponge full of vinegar being pressed to His parched lips. "Marah" might well be written across these closing moments of His sufferings.

THIRTY-FOUR: IT IS FINISHED

"It is finished" (John 19:30)

Matthew, Mark and Luke all tell us that the Lord cried out with a loud voice before giving up His spirit. It is John who tells us that He cried, "It is finished". In the Greek it has a ring of triumph about it: 'Tetelestai!' His work of salvation was perfect and complete so that nothing more needs to be done. In His memorable prayer of review of His earthly labours, the Lord Jesus speaks to His Father as though all things have been accomplished: "I glorified Thee on the earth, having accomplished the work which Thou hast given Me to do" (John 17:4). Only a matter of hours awaited the literal fulfilment of His words, when He was to become the great Sin-purger. All the demands of a holy God were met at Calvary. There sin, Satan and hell were all defeated. Salvation, justification and eternal life are now freely available to every sinful person. One has explained that the Greek sculptor would cry, "Tetelestai!" when his work was finished; no finishing touches necessary; nothing more needing to be done.

"Christ has done the mighty work;

Nothing left for us to do

But to enter on His toil,

Enter on His triumph too."

"Father, into Thy hands I commend My spirit" (Luke 23:46)

Christ's work upon the Cross began and ended with a cry to His Father. The wondrous eternal relationship remained unbroken. The moment has now come when the waiting Father receives the offered spirit of His Son. Heaven must have been hushed when this remarkable happening took place. Men were waiting to put an end to His life; the Father waited for Him to bow His holy head and dismiss His spirit. Voluntarily He laid down His life; voluntarily He gave up His Spirit. No man took His life from Him. The soldier pierced His side, and out flowed blood and water. A centurion glorified God saying, "Certainly this was a righteous Man" (Luke 23:47). And the closing scenes reveal multitudes smiting their breasts when they beheld the things which were done.

"The One who suffered grief and shame

Is raised and glorified.

We sing the triumph of His name,

Who groaned and bled and died."

THIRTY-FIVE: ONE DAY WE'LL UNDERSTAND (PART ONE)

There are many shades of meaning in the word "understand", but the one which concerns us most here is that of gentle thoughts and feelings for one another. There is such a great need for this in the troubling days of stress and sorrow we are now sharing, and perhaps our hearts need to be touched, awakened, appealed to, for such helpful understanding which will help to ease the burden so many are bearing. This is a special message of ministry, then, on behalf of those of God's people passing through the furnace of affliction. Some are in the throes of sickness, bringing with it the anxiety of long-term treatment; others are knowing the deep sorrow of bereavement; while others are experiencing family problems which appear to have no solution; and not a few have known disappointments and set-backs for reasons which remain inexplicable. It may just seem at the present time that our "Days are filled with sorrow and care, Hearts are lonely and drear."

Joy perhaps seems at its ebbtide; no man cares; refuge seems to have failed us (Psalm 142:4). Like David we have cried, made supplication, poured out our complaint, and showed before the Lord our trouble (w.1,2). Bewilderment replaces understanding; anxiety displaces peace; depression overtakes joy. Sometimes we feel absolutely alone in all that is taking place, overwhelmed by the feeling that "it must only be happening to me. And why?" This is the time when help is most needed from those who have been through a similar experience; those who can show empathy, a fellow feeling, as well as sympathy; Those who can provide practical help and understanding. It is wrong to assume, of course, that we are the only ones whose lives seem to be touched. We are not alone in this, and invariably we discover people who are in far worse circumstances than ourselves.

The amount of fruitful service for God which comes from the apparent lonely winepress of human affliction is a marvel in itself. Blindness did not hinder Fanny Crosby from writing some 5,000 hymns. It is said that she withheld one to be published after her death, and that was entitled, "Some day the silver cord will break". Through the mist of her many years of infirmity, she looked for the clear day when "I shall see Him face to face".

A frail, sickly body housed the glowing, devoted spirit of Frances Ridley Havergal, for a mere 40 years; but during that time she poured out thousands of precious thoughts in prose and poetry. The man who wrote "Man of Sorrows", P.P. Bliss, died with his wife in a train accident at the age of 38. His work here had been counted complete by God in half a lifetime. William Cowper suffered so severely from melancholic depression during his Christian life, that he attempted to commit suicide on one occasion. He ordered a London "Cabbie" to drive him to the Thames Embankment where he intended drowning himself in the river. At the commencement of the journey a thick fog surrounded the area, but the driver proceeded and ultimately stopped at what he thought was the embankment. Cowper got out of the cab and found to his consternation that he was back at his own doorstep. He attributed his deliverance to God's intervention, which prompted him to write the hymn which has been blessed to so many Christians:

"God moves in a mysterious way,

His wonders to perform;

He plants His footsteps in the sea,

And rides upon the storm."

It was said to be one of the last of his hymns before he became totally incapacitated. Two other verses say:

"Ye fearful saints, fresh courage take;

The clouds ye so much dread

Are big with mercy, and shall break

In blessings on your head.

Judge not the Lord by feeble sense,

But trust Him for His grace;

Behind a frowning Providence

He hides a smiling face."

THIRTY-SIX: ONE DAY WE'LL UNDERSTAND (PART TWO)

At no time will God give us burdens greater than we can bear; or try us beyond our strength. Peter speaks of Christians being put through manifold trials for a little while as a proof of their faith (1 Peter 1:6). Paul mentions some whose joy increased as the result of their affliction (2 Corinthians 8:2). And the apostle himself had to endure during his lifetime a troublesome thorn in the flesh, which the Lord refused to remove. With it He gave Paul the promise, "My grace is sufficient for thee: for My power is made perfect in weakness" (2 Corinthians 12:9).

God's purpose in putting us through the varied experiences of life is for our own benefit, and so that we can be a help to others. We do not always understand what is happening to us and to others, so we must trust Him as the One who knows the end from the beginning (Isaiah 46:10). We must cry out in faith, "Lord, Thou knowest all things" (John 21:17). It was to the man who made that confession that the Lord said in the Upper Room, "What I do thou knowest not now; but thou shalt understand hereafter" (John 13:7). It referred to one incident only in Peter's life, but it is a sound principle on which faith can rest at all times. Our God is too loving to be unkind; and too wise to make a mistake. Let us seek out those who need comfort and courage, and bear one another's burdens (Galatians 6:2). It is a work of love. It is fulfilling the desire of the great Burden-Bearer Himself; the One who showed unmatched compassion, mercy, and encouragement when needed.

In heaven He continues that very same work for His people today. "For we have not a High Priest that cannot be touched with the feeling of our infirmities; but One that hath been in all points tempted like as we are, yet without sin. Let us therefore draw near with boldness unto the throne of grace" (Hebrews 5:15,16). It is in these verses we get our English word sympathy. The Greek word 'sumpathesai' is translated as 'be touched with the feeling of". What is true of the Man in the Glory should be true of His people on earth. How deep is my sympathy, my understanding, for my brother, for my sister? Deep enough to seek them out? To draw near to them with help and encouragement?

"Not now, but in the coming years,

It may be in the better land,

We'll read the meaning of our tears,

And there, some time, we'll understand.

We'll know why clouds instead of sun

Were over many a cherished plan;

Why song has ceased when scarce begun;

'Tis there, some time, we'll understand.

Then trust in God through all thy days;

Fear not, for He doth hold thy hand;

Though dark thy way, still sing and praise;

Some time, some time, we'll understand."

THIRTY-SEVEN: THE BATTLE, THE MOUNT AND THE TENT

These were the places where a young man learned about the power of God, the glory of God, and the presence of God. The young man was Joshua. He came from Ephraim, and if his tribe had sought the power, the glory, and the divine Presence as Joshua did, their black page of history might never have been written. Joshua was a prince of a man (Numbers 13:2); a leader (Numbers 26:17); a spiritual shepherd (Numbers 26:17); valorous (Joshua 5:13); enduring (Numbers 26:65); obedient (Joshua 4:1-4); diligent (Joshua 7:16-26); and a warrior (Joshua 5:13). In contrast, his descendants were described, at various times, as drunkards (Isa 28:1); deceitful (Hosea 7:16); half baked (Hosea 7:8); like silly doves (Hosea 7:11); those who turned back in the day of battle (Psalm 78:9).

Knowing these characteristics would reveal themselves, God passed over Ephraim and chose Judah as the sovereign tribe (Psalm 78:67-72). However, because of His everlasting love, He will yet make Ephraim as a mighty man (Zechariah 10:7); and as watchers on the hills of Ephraim to cry out to their Millennial brethren, "Arise ye, and let us go up to Zion unto the LORD our God" (Jeremiah 31:1-6). If Ephraim was once passed over by God, it was not so with Joshua. Newly arrived out of Egypt with His chosen people, he was appointed by Moses to arm and lead an Israeli force against Amalek.

This was the baptism of fire for young Joshua. He performed admirably, and Amalek was prostrated (Exodus 17:8-13). Being a Spirit-controlled man (Numbers 27:18), Joshua would attribute victory to the power of the same God who performed miracles in Egypt, and parted the mighty waves of the Red Sea to admit His people into the wilderness. This narrative also confirms what God can do when four of His leaders, Moses, Aaron, Hur, and Joshua, are prepared to sacrifice, endure weariness, and hold on prayerfully with faith in their God.

After seeing such a manifestation of divine power, Joshua must have been awe-struck when he ascended the mount with Moses (Exodus 24:12-18). Here, Joshua the young warrior becomes Moses' servant, and he is given precedence over Aaron, Hur, and the 70 elders, as he accompanies Moses who is to receive the tablets of stone from the hand of God. If the appearance of the glory of the Lord was like devouring fire to Israel, how solemnizing it must have been to young Joshua. During this time, God also gave to Moses the pattern of the Tabernacle. Joshua saw not only the glory of God, but was associated with the vision of the heavenly house, of which Israel was to build a copy on the desert sands.

Our final glimpse of Joshua is in the Tent of meeting where his master, Moses, met with God. This was the place where Joshua quietly observed Moses' life of communion with God. What a privilege for Joshua to witness the pleadings of Israel's great intercessor! To share in the holy joy of hearing God speak to His friend! What an education to share in the secret things which belong unto the Lord our God (Deuteronomy 29:29)! This was the place for Joshua to learn. "Joshua, the son of Nun, a young man, departed not out of the Tent" (Exodus 33:11). Joshua's experiences were all part of God's preparation of the man who was to succeed Moses. These experiences were reinforced over the years, and when the need arose he was able to speak forcefully to the nation in these words: "Fear the LORD, and serve Him in sincerity and in truth ... choose you this day whom ye will serve ... but as for me and my house, we will serve the LORD" (Joshua 24:14,15).

Is there a message in all this for young men of God today? We hope so. One generation comes, and another goes; and if the Truth is to be maintained, then spiritual young men must equip themselves in preparation for the responsibilities of upholding the teachings of the house of God. Paul wrote to a young man of God in his day, these words: "And the things which thou hast heard from me among many witnesses, the same commit thou to faithful men, who shall be able to teach others also" (2 Timothy 2:2). Faithful men; teachers; lovers of souls; lovers of the Scriptures; good soldiers of Jesus Christ; young men of prayer, of vision, of communion. The call will now come with increasing urgency for the young Joshuas to rise up and lead God's people. Experiences in the battle of life, on the mount, and in the tent, can equip them to do this.

THIRTY-EIGHT: THE BABBLER OF ATHENS

"Babbler", that is what they called him. It was a word with a sardonic twist to it. It was meant to be sarcastic, caustic, because they were somewhat anxious about this person in their midst. His message was new and unusual without question; he was a personality; his words carried weight and conviction; and obviously he was not without education. But they had to find a way to humiliate him, so they called him "a babbler", and they brought him by force before their judges.

The man was Paul, the people were Greeks, and the place was Athens. Paul had been shocked at finding the city full of idols of gold, silver, and stone. Then he came across an altar with the inscription, "TO AN UNKNOWN GOD". For a nation which had contributed so much light to the world in arts, sciences, and philosophies, these things indicated deep spiritual darkness. And their only hope, Paul knew, was the gospel of God concerning His Son. It was after he had reasoned on this subject with the Athenian Jews, and encountered the philosophic Epicureans and Stoics, that some enquired, "What would this babbler say?" (Acts 17:18). The Greeks knew the cruelty of this insinuation for their word for "babbler" is "spermologos", a collector of seeds. But it was used derogatively of people who hung about the streets and marketplace picking up scraps like crows. Such persons were classified as parasites, or hangers on; or those who picked up scraps of information and relayed them to groups and crowds in order to put on a show. They were likened to pedlars of second-hand thoughts, plagiarists.

This, then, was the opinion that some of the Athenians held of Paul after he had told them of Jesus and the resurrection (Acts 17:18,19). Surely they had underestimated this man of God; and obviously they were unaware of his background. Jewish born and named Saul of Tarsus, he was exceedingly well-educated, steeped in the law, knowledgeable as to their own poets, a leader of his own nation. But above all this, he had had an experience with Christ which many might envy; an experience he never tired of relating.

Paul had been unable to accept that Jesus of Nazareth was the Messiah. His death on the cross was surely the end of Him, until His disciples began testifying publicly of having seen and heard Him after His resurrection. Then, following Pentecost, a small band of disciples had grown into a multitude, and were still multiplying. It was then that Saul of Tarsus became a vicious persecutor and a murderer of Christians. It was as he journeyed on one of these wild escapades of venomous hatred that he met the risen Christ; it was on the road to Damascus, and Saul was brought to his knees. "Saul, Saul, why persecutest thou Me?" a Voice from heaven asked him. "Who art thou, Lord?" he responded. "I am Jesus whom thou persecutest", answered the Lord Jesus from heaven (Acts 9:3-7).

At that moment, Saul was enlightened by the incontrovertible truth that the Jesus of Calvary must be alive, for He was speaking to him from heaven. Saul needed no more persuading. He arose from the ground a new man, born again, and the Lord's vindictive opponent became His faithful follower. He became the standard bearer of the faith; he proclaimed the complete gospel, which he described as "the power of God unto salvation to every one that believeth" (Romans 1:16); he encouraged those who were born again to become disciples of the Lord Jesus, to be baptized, and added to a church of God. He had the vision of churches of God forming a house for God, and he did not tire in proclaiming this heavenly vision. He was faithful to the end of his life as a good soldier of Jesus Christ, a faithful contender in the spiritual race, and a guardian of the truth. This was no babbler, but a true servant of the God of heaven.

So before the elite of Athens, in the place where Socrates once stood, Paul gave his masterly presentation of divine truth. He chastised the Athenians for their superstition and ignorance; he emphasized the existence of God and His creatorial work; the dependence of men upon Him, and His Personal nearness to men; he warned of a day of judgement decreed by God for those who disobeyed His commandment to repent, and the Judge would be His Son - Christ crucified and risen from the dead. This Spirit-guided message caused some to mock, others to postpone their decision, but a few to believe and become followers of the Man of Calvary (Acts 17:22-34).

We can all learn a profitable lesson from this experience of Paul when he ignored the jeers and disdainful remarks, and found great consolation in the outcome of his message. It is recorded for eternity that "certain men clave unto him, and believed: among whom also was Dionysius the Areopagite, and a woman named Damaris, and others with them" (v.34). What does it matter what men say about us as long as we are faithful in presenting the truth of God? He has promised "... My word ... shall not return unto Me void, but it shall accomplish that which I please" (Isaiah 55:11).

THIRTY-NINE: THE DAY IT WAS BROKEN

It was a custom in Eastern lands of ancient days to "save" precious oil, and "bank" it in alabaster vases or boxes. The alabaster stone, semi-transparent in appearance, could be highly polished and skillfully made into vessels of varying forms. Apothecaries used these vessels for storing medicines and perfumes; but some people would buy from the apothecary a measure of precious oil to put into an "enclosed" container, and add to it as they prospered. Only when the vase was full would it be sealed by the apothecary, and the person would keep this most valuable investment for the occasion for which it was intended.

This appeared to be the case with the loving, worshipping, nameless woman in the Bethany home of Simon the leper (Mark 14). She had brought with her an alabaster cruse of very costly (v.3), fragrant nard, which had likely accumulated over a long period of time. After its sealing, she had kept it for that memorable day when she would anoint her Lord in anticipation of His death and burial (v.8). What foresight and faith she had. That day had now arrived, and in His presence she broke the seal, and poured the precious oil over His head (v.3). The house would be filled with the odour of the perfume; none would escape its effect, and they would carry it with them, willingly or unwillingly, wherever they went. We sometimes overlook, the fact that this dear woman was herself a vessel filled with fragrant adoration and worship for her Lord and Messiah King. That day, too, she was broken, and there flowed out to Him her deep love, gratitude, and devotion.

But our record would be incomplete without reference to the great outpouring of a loving, kind, and considerate God. The remarkable incident in Simon's home was a pale reflection of what God Himself did from Genesis to Malachi. It was just as though He took His own cruse, and kept adding to it all the fragrant, prophetic utterances concerning His Son, until the time came when it had to be broken. The first drop into the divine vessel was that word of hope and victory, after sin had entered into the world, that the Seed of the woman would bruise the serpent's head (Genesis 3:15). Later was added, "God will provide Himself the Lamb for the burnt offering" (Genesis 22:8). Afterwards He went on to gather in succession the fragrant tributes by His prophets to the Coming One:

> From Moses: "The LORD thy God will raise up unto thee a prophet ... unto Him shall ye hearken" (Deuteronomy 18:15).
>
> From David: "The LORD is my shepherd" (Psalm 23:1).
>
> The sons of Korah add their drops: "thou art fairer than the children of men; Grace is poured into Thy lips" (Psalm 45:2).
>
> Then into the cruse is poured Isaiah's tribute: "... Unto us a Child is born, unto us a Son is given ... and His name shall be called Wonderful, Counsellor, Mighty God, Everlasting Father, Prince of Peace" (9:6).
>
> Micah is next: "Be thou, Bethlehem Ephrathah ... out of thee shall One come forth ... that is to be Ruler in Israel" (Micah 5:2).

Then the final, fragrant drop from Malachi: "... until you that bear My name shall the Sun of righteousness arise with healing in His wings" (Malachi 4:2).

Then comes the time for the divine hand to seal the flask, and to keep it against the great day of its breaking and pouring out. Some 400 years must pass before the blessed announcement of the miraculous birth of Bethlehem; the seal had been broken, and there poured forth the fragrant, precious proclamation: "and thou shalt call His name JESUS" (Matthew 1:21). "Thy name is as ointment, poured forth", said the beloved one (Song of Songs 1:3), and our redeemed hearts respond, "Amen, Amen".

"And hast Thou, Lord, some little task for me?

Such as I am - that I may do for Thee?

Unworthy, sin-born, sin-bred, yet Thou hast

Named me among Thy workers; and my past

That ne'er recorded aught for Thee of good,

Obliterated by Thy precious blood.

The wonder is, that I, of sinful race,

Have been (Oh token of Thy sov'reign grace)

Entrusted with so hon'rable a place!

Lord, teach me, fit me, aid me, so I may

Out from this life save something for "that day",

Rich with the savour of that peerless Name;

Deemed to enhance Thine everlasting fame." (C. Belton)

FORTY: CLIMB! (PART ONE)

That was the command given by General Wolfe when he came to Canada to conquer Quebec. His attack was to be made unexpectedly from the Heights of Abraham, the scaling of which was a formidable task. "Climb, and keep climbing", Wolfe instructed his men. "I do not know if this will succeed, but we must keep trying". Wolfe's mountain men succeeded in their endeavour, and victory was assured. God, too, has His mountain men. From Abraham onwards, God encouraged His servants to climb mountains. Sometimes this was His plan of preparation in order that crises which lay ahead could be met effectively. In the Scriptures the mountain is a place of worship (Genesis 12:8); of proving (Genesis 22:1); of blessing (Psalm 133:3); of teaching (Matthew 5:1,2); of choosing (Mark 3:13,14); of revelation (Luke 9:28-36); of commission (Matthew 28:16); and of ascension (Acts 1:6-12).

After Abram entered Canaan, he climbed a mountain and pitched his tent between Bethel ("the house of God") and Ai ("ruins") "and there he builded an altar unto the Lord" (Genesis 12:8). It was to this very spot that Abram returned after his lapse of faith, when he went down into Egypt where troubles pursued him. He must have been glad to leave Egypt. There was no revealed purpose of God in him being there, and it is good to read that he came up out of Egypt, "And he went ... unto the place where his tent had been at the beginning, between Bethel and Ai; unto the place of the altar, which he had made there at the first" (Genesis 13:1-4). It is a great encouragement to read of a man returning to the place where he had dealings with God although it demands a mountain climb. Abram, a man of the tent and altar, knew the value of worshipping God and of communion with Him, for himself and his family.

One day Abram would climb the highest of his mountains in order to be tested by God. Mount Moriah would be the place of supreme sacrifice, for there Abram would be asked to offer his darling son Isaac. Abram obeyed and, honouring his obedience, God intervened at the crucial moment. True to His Name, Jehovah Jireh, He provided a ram as a substitute for Isaac. This points us to Calvary, yet another mountain, where God would allow His Son to be sacrificed without any divine intervention. Christ would be the Lamb and the Ram.

FORTY-ONE: CLIMB! (PART TWO)

Unquestionably Moses is the mountain man of Scripture. His climbs would be excelled only by the Lord Jesus. After his flight from Egypt, Moses spent 40 years in the wilderness as a shepherd, a task which was an abomination to the Egyptians (Genesis 46:34). It was while he cared for the flock at Horeb, the mountain of God, that he saw the burning bush. To Moses it was "this great sight". He must have seen many remarkable things in Egypt, but none compared with a bush which burned and was not consumed. "And the angel of the LORD appeared unto him in a flame of fire out of the midst of a bush... And ... God called unto him out of the midst of the bush" (Exodus 3:1-4).

Moses would never forget the divine command, "Draw not nigh hither: put off thy shoes from off thy feet, for the place whereon thou standest is holy ground" (Exodus 3:5). The man who had known his every want and wish answered by servants in Pharaoh's palace, whose shoes would be removed and replaced by the same humble servants, must now take off his own shoes in preparation for getting down to the level of help needed by God's downtrodden people in Egypt. What he saw on the mountain was an assurance that Israel would pass through fiery trials, but would be preserved by God through them all; and what he heard, "I will send thee unto Pharaoh" (3:10), was the beginning of a great work which would culminate in a holy nation being formed for God, and a tabernacle being built for God in the wilderness.

It was on another mountain, Sinai, that he would receive God's instructions for this. Although Moses was denied the privilege of leading Israel into the promised land, because of his own misdemeanour, he was permitted to view it from Mount Nebo; but better still he was allowed into the land in somewhat startling fashion when he appeared on yet another mount, the holy mount, as Peter described it, or the mount of Transfiguration. There he stood with Elijah and the Lord Jesus, an unforgettable scene witnessed by Peter, James and John (Luke 9:28-36), nevertheless a scene which was a fitting conclusion for a man who so often dwelt on the mountain with God.

FORTY-TWO: FIVE THINGS (PART ONE)

The fragrance of a rose, the smell of crushed grapes, the odour of pine needles, all come from the Hand of our great Creator, and they excel by far the synthetic equivalents produced by man. Our God is a God of fragrances, and they have a place of highest importance in the service and worship of His house. Five ingredients were all the Creator required for blending together to provide the fragrant, holy oil for use in the divine dwelling-place. And it was only in connection with His holy nation that God decreed that this oil should be used.

There were seven important parts of the tabernacle in the wilderness which had to be anointed with the specially prepared oil which the Lord instructed Moses to have made. They were the tent of meeting, the ark of testimony, the table of shewbread, the lampstand, the altar of incense, the altar of burnt offering, and the laver (Exodus 30:26-28). All the vessels of the house, and Aaron and his sons, were also anointed with this fragrant oil, which is called holy (v.25), and precious (Psalm 133:2).

The five things chosen by God for the holy anointing oil were myrrh, cinnamon, calamus, cassia, and olive oil, and they were compounded by one of Israel's skilled perfumers (Exodus 30:25). Anyone found producing an imitation, or using it upon one who did not belong to God's people, was banished from the holy nation (v.33). It would seem that the holy anointing oil typifies the fragrant virtues of the Person of Christ as revealed by the Holy Spirit. The Lord Jesus promised His disciples that the Spirit of truth "shall glorify Me: for He shall take of Mine, and shall declare it unto you" (John 16:14). And to the two on the road to Emmaus He began "from Moses and from all the prophets", and "interpreted to them in all the scriptures the things concerning Himself" (Luke 24:27). Concerning the first two ingredients, therefore, we would offer the following suggestive thoughts as to their typical teaching.

MYRRH was a bitter gum derived from the leaves of a thorn-bearing tree, which was found in abundance on the hillsides of Palestine. Myrrh was often used as a gift to kings and dignitaries. It was one of the gifts of the wise men to the Lord Jesus as a child (Matthew 2:11). They came seeking the king (v.2), and they brought gifts befitting a king. The gold indicated His divine glory; the white frankincense suggested the pure, fragrant life He lived; and the myrrh could be indicative of His suffering in life and in death. There was myrrh given at His birth and at His burial (John 19:39). These were noble tributes to the King, albeit He was despised and rejected. The thorn-bearing tree, the piercing of the leaves to produce the gum, and the bitterness of it, would speak to our redeemed souls of the mocker's crown, the wounded hands and feet, and "the bitter sorrows that He bore". Finally, the gum had to be gathered, revealing the need for us to gather in our quiet moments of reading and meditation, precious thoughts of the One who endured the cross, despising its shame (Hebrews 12:2).

CINNAMON was obtained from the inner bark of an aromatic tree of the laurel family, and this would remind us of the fragrant life of Christ known to His Father alone. Every single thought of His was so pure and holy, and came from a mind undefiled by sin. How God delighted in His Son, and the times of sweet communion they enjoyed together! Men were privileged to see His miracles, and hear His gracious words, but at no time were they permitted to intrude on the privacy of those hours on the mountain when His locks were filled with the dew of the night. Luke tells us that He "went out into the mountain to pray; and He continued all night in prayer to God" (Luke 6:12). Jeremiah mentions repeatedly that the heart of man is evil, but in contrast Peter fitly describes the inner life of the Lord with these words: "who did no sin, neither was guile found in His mouth" (1 Peter 2:22). The cinnamon tree often grew to be 30 feet high, and it commanded attention because of its height, and its value. So with our Lord Jesus who is "high and lifted up" in our esteem; He is deserving of all honour, praise, and value, and He is worthy of the highest place which He now occupies in heaven.

FORTY-THREE: FIVE THINGS (PART TWO)

Here are some meditations on two more of the five fragrances. CALAMUS was brought to Palestine from distant lands, was regarded highly for its sweetness, and became known commonly as sweet cane. These considerations give rise to two precious thoughts concerning Christ. Firstly, He came from the bosom of Divinity to the bosom of humanity; "And the Word became flesh, and dwelt among us" (John 1:14); "I am the bread of life This is the bread which cometh down out of heaven, that a man may eat thereof, and not die" (John 6:48,50). He virtually stepped down from the throne of heaven; crossed the bridge of eternity to enter the stream of humanity; to receive not a crown but a cross. He was, indeed, the sweet calamus from a distant land. Men "wondered at the words of grace which proceeded out of His mouth" (Luke 4:22). But His beloved provides the answer to their perplexity in these words, "His mouth (or speech) is most sweet: Yea, he is altogether lovely. This is my beloved, and this is my friend" (Song of Songs 5:16). Calamus was one of the chief spices (Song of Songs 4:14), and is included with ivory, ebony, emeralds, and rubies, in the list of valuables carried by the merchants' caravans. Our hearts would respond: "My beloved Isaiah ... The chiefest among ten thousand" (Song of Songs 5:10).

CASSIA is of uncertain origin, but came apparently from the outer bark of a tree, or was stripped from a violet-scented root. In the Hebrew, cassia derives from words meaning "to stoop, bow down, peel, stripping". In considering the similarity of each of these features, there forms a consistent pattern of devotional truth concerning Christ. The outer bark is suggestive of His fragrant life before men, in contrast to the inner bark of the cinnamon indicating His inner life before God. There is a universal tribute to the perfect life of Christ' on earth, in this fourfold tribute. His Father said, "Thou art My beloved Son, in Thee I am well pleased" (Mark 1:11). The demon cried, "I know thee who thou art, the Holy One of God" (Luke 4:34). Pilate said, "I ... found no fault in this man (Luke 23:14). The centurion declared, "Certainly this was a righteous man" (Luke 23:47).

The "stoop" and "bowing down" immediately suggest the humility of the Son of God in coming to earth. To the Corinthians Paul said, "For ye know the grace of our Lord Jesus Christ, that, though He was rich, yet for your sakes He became poor, that ye through His poverty might become rich" (2 Corinthians 8:9). To the Philippians he wrote: "... Christ Jesus: who, being in the form of God, counted it not a prize to be on an equality with God, but emptied Himself, taking the form of a servant, being made in the likeness of men; ... He humbled Himself... becoming obedient even unto death, yea the death of the cross" (2:6,8). These words are self-illuminating, and require no comment. Christ bowed to the will of His Father in implicit obedience (Luke 22:42); and He was bowed down by the weight of the cross where He was to become "obedient unto death". He willingly laid down His life. Even the stripping of the bark or root is yet another reminder of the mockery with the purple robe, the crown of thorns, the reed. They may have stripped His garments, but they could not take away His dignity or eternal love. This He manifested in His gracious prayer, "Father, forgive them; for they know not what they do" (Luke 23:34). "Hallelujah! What a Saviour!"

FORTY-FOUR: FIVE THINGS (PART THREE)

And so we come to meditating on the fifth of the fragrances. OLIVE OIL, mentioned over 200 times in Scripture, came from one of earth's earliest trees (Genesis 8:11). The olives grew in abundance, and they were pressed to produce the valuable oil of high quality. It is a type of the Holy Spirit as seen from the following uses. In the parable the wise virgins used it in their lamps to provide light (Matthew 25), illustrating our need of the Spirit in individual testimony. "He ... shall be in you" (John 14:17). In the lampstand it was used for light in God's house, speaking of the Spirit's work in a church of God (Revelation 1:20). For anointing David in the midst of his brethren (1 Samuel 16:13), and so sanctifying him for God's purpose, even as we have anointing of the Holy One which abides in us (1 John 2:20,27).

So the chief spices were blended together with the pure olive oil to produce one sweet, fragrant holy anointing oil for the Lord, His people, and His house. The perfumer took the individual ingredients and united them according to divine direction. Unity in the Spirit must always be God's way (Ephesians 4:3), and this is something we are instructed to keep, and we can if we bow to His instruction as He reveals Christ to us. "He shall guide you into all the truth" (John 16:13); "He shall glorify Me: for He shall take of Mine, and shall declare it unto you" (v.14). The oil was to be used only where the Lord ordained, and it was to be used liberally. "... God ... giveth not the Spirit by measure" (John 3:34). Who can limit the virtues of Christ? There is no thought of sprinkling the oil, but rather a pouring out. David confirms this in describing that the unity of brethren is like the precious oil upon the head, the beard, and the garments of Aaron (Psalm 133:1). It "ran down upon the beard" (v.2). It was quiet in its operation, just as the dew of Hermon descended silently.

The sweetness of harmony on the part of brethren answers to the blending of the virtues of Christ by the Spirit. "For there the LORD commanded the blessing, even life for evermore" (v.3). Could it be that David is showing us in this Song of Ascents that the Lord will command His blessing where brethren dwell together in unity? If so, it is a precious thought. Let us be encouraged to look up to heaven's throne where God has anointed His Son "with the oil of gladness above Thy fellows" (Hebrews 1:9). He has fellows, we are in His Fellowship where that unity can be expressed.

FORTY-FIVE: THE IMPORTANCE OF OBEDIENCE

An unusual altar appeared in the midst of Israel one day, and it was not long before it was given pre-eminence over the altar of God. Where did it originate? Who was the maker? Ahaz, the ruler of Judah, and father of good king Hezekiah, went to Damascus on a visit to the king of Assyria. There he saw an altar that took his fancy. Possibly it had many attractive features, and he thought it would add to the decor of the court of God's dwelling. So he sent a pattern of it to Urijah the priest, and instructed him to make one like it. When Ahaz arrived home the new altar was ready, and he "drew near unto the altar, and offered thereon" (2 Kings 16:12). Burnt offerings, meal offerings and drink offerings, were all offered by king Ahaz, and he also sprinkled the blood of his peace offerings upon the altar (v.13). But no mention is made of a sin offering.

Then came the time when the brazen altar of the Lord was moved out of its place, and the Assyrian altar, which Ahaz now called his altar (v.14), became the great altar (v.15). On it Urijah offered the sacrifices of all the people of the land. "Thus did Urijah the priest, according to all that king Ahaz commanded" (v.16); but certainly not according to what the Lord commanded. This story is surely a warning to us today of the ease with which things foreign to God and His word can be brought into His house. Ahaz and others might have rationalized that it was a beautiful altar he had seen in Assyria, and that it was a good idea to introduce it into Israel. More sacrifices could now be offered with an additional altar. But it must never be forgotten that the house belongs to God, and He must decree what is to be done there.

In connection with the Tabernacle in the wilderness Moses was warned, "See ... that thou make all things according to the pattern that was shewed thee in the mount" (Hebrews 8:5). This makes it abundantly clear that although God gave to consecrated men and women the responsibility for the making of the house and its furniture, He alone was the Architect and Designer. For the building of the Temple, it is written that king David gave the pattern to his son Solomon (1 Chronicles 2811), and concerning it David said, "All this ... have I been made to understand in writing from the hand of the LORD, even all the works of this pattern ... Be strong and of good courage, and do it" (vv.19,20). Although Moses, David and Solomon were all capable, wise, and godly men, they were not allowed to introduce any of their own ideas into the building of God's dwelling. It is important for us to be aware that what men do in Christendom today, with the best intentions in the world, can be without the Lord's authority. Plans, programmes, and techniques are devised, and many things introduced to attract people, which are contrary to the Scriptures. But we are in the place of divine authority, and are no part of Christendom where men's ideas are followed without compunction. We must be obedient to His word.

FORTY-SIX: DAVID'S VISION FOR GOD'S HOUSE

The deep devotion and affection for the house of God shown by David are unsurpassed by any other man of God in the Scriptures. The theme of the house of the Lord was not only on his lips constantly, but was also engraved on his heart. Not all are aware that it was David who first said, "The zeal of Thine house hath eaten me up" (Psalm 69:9), and these words reflect the prime place the divine dwelling had in his life. He was a man of the house, and a man of the altar, who realized that ritual offerings could not replace the sacrifices of God which are "a broken spirit: a broken and a contrite heart, O God, Thou wilt not despise" (Psalm 51:17). He was a man of prayer and worship, who rejoiced to lead the throng "to the house of God, with the voice of joy and praise" (Psalm 42:4).

Israel's monarch showed clearly by his words and actions that God and His house are indivisible, and in his psalms he tells of his love for both. When he was delivered from Saul, and a host of other antagonists, David sang, "I love Thee, O LORD, my strength ... my rock, and my fortress" (Psalm 18:1,2). When he observed the foul deeds of evil men around him with their bribes, mischief and murders, he walked a separated path from them, and cried out with rejoicing: "LORD, I love the habitation of Thy house, and the place where Thy glory dwelleth. My foot standeth in an even place: in the congregations will I bless the LORD" (Psalm 26:8,12). The love which David had for God's house is wondrously revealed in his vision, his provision, and his determination; precious examples for all who are in the place of the Name today.

It has been said that vision is sight plus light. It is the opposite to blindness and darkness. A blind person who had an implicit faith in God was once asked what she considered to be the worst tragedy which could befall her, and she replied, "To have sight but no vision". David was a man of vision. His concept of a divine dwelling-place can only be measured by the concept he had of the majesty and sovereignty of the God he loved and worshipped. "The house that is to be builded must be exceeding magnifical, of fame and of glory" (1 Chronicles 22:5); it was to be a palace, not for man, but for the LORD God (1 Chronicles 29:1). David wanted to build a place for the King of glory to enter into; a place where the King of ages would in very deed dwell with men, and so he prepared accordingly.

Can David's vision of such a house for God elevate our spiritual understanding too? Yes, and it must if we are to appreciate fully the great thing God has done for us in making us living stones, which He has built into His spiritual house where we can worship and serve Him in love, as a holy and royal priesthood (1 Peter 2:3-9). Men speak of the seven wonders of the world, but to David there was only one wonder, and that was a majestic, amiable (lovely, unique), dwelling for "My King, and my God" (Psalm 84:1,3).

FORTY-SEVEN: DAVID'S SUBMISSION TO GOD'S HOUSE

We don't for a moment suggest that David belittled, despised, or downgraded the tabernacle which existed at the time he disclosed to Nathan the prophet his desire to build a house for God. It was an active conscience which prompted him to say to the prophet, "See now, I dwell in a house of cedar, but the ark of God dwelleth within curtains" (2 Samuel 7:1,2). David was at peace, and was resting on the laurels which God had given him after many battles, and he saw the discrepancy between his own dwelling and that of the Lord.

There was nothing wrong with the tabernacle which David wanted to replace. After all, it had been made with the very best of materials, by the most skilful of hands, and according to the choicest of patterns. This was the very tabernacle in the wilderness which Moses was instructed to build after he had been shown by God that copy and shadow of heavenly things on Mount Sinai. Those same curtains of blue, purple, and scarlet, and fine twined linen; the furniture of acacia wood covered with gold; and the brazen pillars and altar, were all transported under the leadership of Joshua into the promised land (see Acts 7:44-46). God had said to Nathan, "I have not dwelt in a house since the day that I brought up the children of Israel out of Egypt, even to this day, but have walked in a tent and in a tabernacle" (2 Samuel 7:6).

Nathan had told David to do all that was in his heart and to build the house for God (v.3), but God decreed otherwise. The prophet was instructed to tell David of the things which God had done, and would do for him. "Thine house and thy kingdom shall be made sure for ever before thee: thy throne shall be established for ever", said God (2 Samuel 7:16). But Solomon, his son, not David, would have the honour of building the house. "Thou shalt not build a house for My name, because thou art a man of war, and hast shed blood" (1 Chronicles 28:3), David was told by God. The disappointment must have been keenly felt by David, but there was no arguing with the Lord and no protestation; just a humble submission to His will. It is good for us to remember here that it was David who first said, "I delight to do Thy will, O my God; yea, Thy law is within my heart" (Psalm 40:8).

It is a delight to God and His people to see a person bowing to His will, and this is one more important lesson we can learn from David's love for the house of God. It is only through submission to the divine will that we can enter into the great blessing of being part of His collective testimony on earth today. It seems so hard for Christians to accept the conditions which God has laid down in His Word whereby we may become part of His house, but the Holy Spirit will enable us to see the vision if we are prepared to be like David by not questioning the wisdom, the love and the purpose of His divine plan for all believers in this dispensation. "If any man willeth to do His will, he shall know of the teaching" (John 7:17). Willing-hearted people helped to make the tabernacle in the wilderness (Exodus 35:20-29), and God seeks such today.

FORTY-EIGHT: DAVID'S PROVISION FOR GOD'S HOUSE

It has been said that "Love ever gives, and because it gives it lives, for this is love's prerogative, to give and give and give". This adequately expresses the desire of David in making available the vast amount of material and wealth needed for the construction of the magnificent palace for the God he loved. We can measure again the extent of David's love for the house of God by the lavishness of his provision. Everything he gave was in abundance. In this he reflected that he was a man after God's heart, for our God is indeed abundant in His giving. How can we ever forget the abundant grace (Romans 5:17), the abundant joy (2 Corinthians 8:2), the abundant mercy (1 Peter 1:3), and the abundant pardon (Isaiah 55:7)? David enjoyed like experiences and so he responded accordingly; perhaps counterbalancing the word which the Lord spoke at the time He advised David he could not build the house. "Thou hast shed blood abundantly", said God, "and hast made great wars" (1 Chronicles 22:8).

Included in the great catalogue of David's provision were a hundred thousand talents each of gold and silver; the brass and iron was too much to weigh; the cedar trees were without number, and so were the precious stones and the marble (1 Chronicles 22:1-6; 29:1-6). Why did David provide so lavishly? The answer is given by the king to his son. "I have prepared with all my might for the house of my God ... also, because I have set my affection to the house of my God, seeing that I have a treasure of mine own of gold and silver, I give it unto the house of my God, over and above all that I have prepared for the holy house"

(1 Chronicles 29:2,3). The man who gave in abundance, who gave "over and above", was the man who could appeal to the nation for volunteers to consecrate themselves willingly to the great undertaking for God. And what a response he received! The princes, the captains, the rulers, offered willingly and gave for the service (vv. 6,7).

Determination

David was conscious, as we all should be, of the time limitation of our lives. Days move by rapidly, and we become concerned about the little we have accomplished in God's house. "Behold, Thou hast made my days as handbreadths; and mine age is as nothing before Thee" (Psalm 39:5), he said. Yet the 70 years he lived were filled with that varied service of a true man of God. There were the times for battle, times for peace, times for worship, times for prayer, times for proclamation to the congregation and times for encouraging others. And amidst it all there were defeats and triumphs, departure and devotion, forgetfulness and remembrance, silence and speaking, despair and cheer.

Yet, the great theme running constantly through that noble heart was expressed in words now known the world over: "Surely goodness and mercy shall follow me all the days of my life; and I will dwell in the house of the LORD for ever" (Psalm 23:6). Here was a sheep content to know the protection and sustaining power of Jehovah Rohi - the Lord is my Shepherd. David's love for the Shepherd-King is seen clearly in this choicest of psalms. That same divine One provides us, too, with His protection and provision in His house today. The great determination of David is also seen in days of trouble and pursuit. Acknowledging the Lord to be his pavilion of secret and tent of safety, he exclaims, "One thing have I asked of the LORD, that will I seek after; that I may dwell in the house of the LORD all the days of my life, to behold the beauty of the LORD, and to inquire in His temple" (Psalm 27:4).

David loved the house because God was there in His glory, because it was a place of prayer, of refuge, a place where the voice of God could be heard. This was true of the divine dwelling of curtains as well as the magnificent temple which Solomon was to build. In the closing Songs of Ascents, we are given yet another glimpse of the determination of the son of Jesse. "I will not come into ... my house, nor go up into my bed; I will not give sleep to mine eyes, or slumber to mine eyelids; until I find out a place for the LORD, a tabernacle for the Mighty One of Jacob" (Psalm 132:3-5). What an example to us is the love, the zeal, the vision, the determination, and the generosity of David! It is worthy of our imitation.

"Who in Thy house abide are blest,

They will be praising still;

And blest is he who, trusting, loves

The ways to Zion's hill.

Joy-springs and blessings mark their path

Along this vale of tears;

With strength renewed before their God

In Zion each appears."

FORTY-NINE: WHY ME?

This is a question Christians should ask themselves frequently in order to preserve in their lives the freshness of the blessing of salvation. A famous preacher was once asked, "Is it not a mystery to you that the Lord chose Judas Iscariot?" And he replied, "It is even a greater mystery that the Lord chose me". Everyone belonging to Christ will gladly endorse this latter statement, but we must take time out of our very busy lives in a very demanding world to dwell on the wonder of God's choice of us to be part of the heavenly family; and that out of those in our family, our neighbourhood, our city, our country, the Lord chose us as individuals for salvation.

It makes for a healthy exercise of soul to ask ourselves the question daily, "Why me, Lord?" David once cried: "... for there is no man that knoweth me ... no man careth for my soul" (Psalm 142:4). We can never say that! Someone - a mother, a father, a brother, a sister, a childhood friend, a Sunday school teacher, or even a preacher - has shown concern for our soul, and told us about Christ. They took time to quote to us the Scriptures; they told us the love story of Calvary; and the gracious Holy Spirit did the rest. Their care for our soul was a reflection of that of the blessed Son of God who cared so deeply that He gave His precious, perfect life in redeeming love on the Cross, in order that we might live with Him and live for Him. But why me? Eternity will reveal the answer to the question.

"Not till the loom is silent,

And the shuttle cease to fly;

Will God unroll the canvas,

And show the reason why."

Till then, let us join the mighty host of witnesses who have marvelled also at the mystery of God's gracious choosing, but have not kept silent about the grace which has saved them and the love which has sustained them. "Declare how great things God hath done for thee" (Luke 8:39).

FIFTY: WHAT AM I?

There is nothing new in the statement that we live in a sad, lonely world. But things do happen sometimes which jolt us into the realization that on our very doorsteps drastic, heart-rending incidents can happen. A story of grief and sorrow must surely lie behind this notice in the obituary column of a prominent newspaper:

UNKNOWN FEMALE - aged approximately 16 years. Funeral service Thursday ... at 9 a.m ... Memorial Chapel ... Interment at ... cemetery...

The girl had been found in a park; she had been murdered. No identification was found; no clues as to parents or birthplace. Just an unknown female. One of the many thousands of this world's children missing from their homes. Doctors, sociologists and police are, at the time of writing, still cataloguing information in their endeavour to find an explanation for this calamitous situation.

How thankful we should be for the opportunity to speak to children about Christ! How vastly important is our work and responsibility in the Sunday school! How necessary it is to impress on children their need of Christ as Saviour and Protector from the world's evil temptations; how helpful and wise we need to be with young Christians who are being bombarded from all sides in a Satan-controlled world! Many will remember that as young people someone cared for us; gave us the fellowship and protection of their homes; taught us the Word, nurtured us, and set us a good example. We must emulate these beloved Christians.

There is one gift given to the Church which can be so easily overlooked. It is tucked away in the verse with apparent insignificance, and yet it is so important. It is classified under the heading of "helps" (1 Corinthians 12:28). We need to ask ourselves by way of examination sometimes: "What am I in the church of God?" and follow it up with two further enquiries, "What can I be?" and, "What would I like to be?" The word "helps" is used only once, and it means to support, to participate with in order to help, to succour, to give relief.

What a valuable work this is - David appreciated the men who helped him from day to day (1 Chronicles 12:21,22); Paul commended by name Urbanus and Priscilla and Aquila as helpers in Christ Jesus (Romans 16:3,9); and he encouraged Epaphroditus to help reconcile the differences between the two sisters in the church at Philippi (Philippians 4:2,3). What am I? A help, helpless, or a hindrance?

FIFTY-ONE: GOOD INTENTIONS

Good intentions are not always good enough, and this David found out to his dismay. When Israel recovered the Ark of the Covenant from the Philistines, David was so overjoyed that he provided a new cart for it to be transported from the house of Abinadab. Knowing David's love for the Lord, we can be sure that the cart was made of the very best materials, and by the very best craftsmen. But this did not prove that it was being done according to the mind of the Lord. All the singing, and the playing with harps, psalteries, timbrels, and cymbals, "with all their might", did not change a wrong action into a right one. The oxen drawing the cart became restive and stumbled, an Israelite, Uzza by name, stretched out his hand to hold the ark, and in a moment the judgement of God came upon him, and Uzza died. David's good intention cost a man his life. God had decreed that none ought to carry the ark of God but the Levites, and David's substitute could not possibly meet with God's approval (1 Chronicles 13:11; 15:2). But this is how these things happen.

What shall we say of the two sons of Aaron, Nadab and Abihu, who each took his censer as ordained priests of Israel, put fire therein, laid incense thereon, and came before the LORD? Everything appeared to be in order, but it was not. They offered what God calls "strange fire". It was of their own making. It was not divine fire which was used to light the altar of burnt offering (see Leviticus 9:24). Did it really matter? After all, fire was being used, and the incense would burn just as fragrantly. God does not ask us to reason and decide what we think is best. He desires hearts that are obedient; disciples who are willing to follow His direction. If Nadab and Abihu did not appreciate the great importance of divine fire, they were learn to their sorrow. Fire from the presence of the Lord immediately devoured them, and their second cousins were chosen to carry their remains in their coats, from before the sanctuary to a place outside the camp (Leviticus 10:1-7).

Do let us take to heart that God wants us to live and build according to His direction. If we learn the secret of this in God's house today, we will be less concerned about what others outside the house are doing.

FIFTY-TWO: AN INSTANT HOUSE

It took only 20 hours to build, and it is a tribute to what men can accomplish through a united effort. Over 300 tradesmen and management personnel were involved in the project. They gave their time, and using donated material they erected a 4-apartment dwelling in a small Canadian town in less than a day. The building of this "instant house" was quite an achievement, and it can be a lesson to God's people as to what can be accomplished through a willing and concerted effort.

Churches of God, of course, are not built in a day. The golden lampstand of the tabernacle teaches us this. The lampstand was of beaten work, and not of molten gold poured into a mould for instant use, as in the case of the humanly devised golden calf (Exodus 32:4). The word "beaten" indicates hammering with skillful lightness or with severity. God chose a man for this work named Bezalel, from the kingly tribe of Judah, and he was "filled with the Spirit of God, in wisdom, in understanding and in knowledge" (Exodus 35:30,31). The lampstand was not of "instant" origin; it took time to make despite the skill, and knowledge, and patience of the craftsman, who began with a solid piece of pure gold over 100 pounds in weight. God in His wisdom did not disclose a size for this beautiful structure.

It is good for us in the house of God today to apply in a practical way the lessons of the golden lampstand. We need to be equipped spiritually with the four qualities that were granted to Bezalel; (1) the filling of the Holy Spirit; (2) wisdom; (3) understanding; and (4) knowledge, if we are to make something of the "gold", the redeemed souls which the Lord brings into our lives.

Through the Spirit we must use the hammer of the Word on the gold to shape it, and this will involve wisdom, understanding and knowledge. It is not a casual, makeshift job, for the work we are doing is that of making disciples. Souls are saved; disciples are made (John 4:1). Our work is not to form meetings of Christians. This is a comparatively easy task, similar to building an "instant house". We have been given the responsibility by the resurrected Lord Jesus to preach the gospel (Mark 16:15), make disciples, baptize them, and teach them (Matthew 28:20). This is what took place on the day of Pentecost when those who were saved and baptized were added together to form a church of God, and they continued steadfastly in the apostles' teaching, in the fellowship, in the breaking of the bread, and in the prayers (Acts 2:41,42). God does not specify how large or how small a church of God should be, in the same way as there is no size given for the lampstand. But we do know that, whatever its size, it is of divine origin.

FIFTY-THREE: LESS THAN ONE PERCENT

Some army generals will go into battle only if they have superiority in numbers of men and equipment. This may be good human planning, but God does not work that way. He is content to achieve His purposes through a minority, showing that He works in strange or paradoxical ways (Luke 5:26). He often does the very opposite to what man would do, and this is one of the divine secrets which we have to learn as Christians.

Gideon might have felt more secure with the original 32,000 to meet the enemy which was likened to a multitude of locusts (Judges 7:12). The number was reduced to 10,000 because the majority went home in fear and trembling (verse 3). The army was still too large for the Lord, and so He whittled it down to 300 proven men (verses 4-9). God needed less than one per cent of the original number to prove His victorious power. After dividing the 300 into three companies, and equipping them with trumpets, empty pitchers and torches - not the most formidable weapons by any means - Gideon spoke these memorable words: "Look on me, and do likewise ... as I do, so shall ye do" (verse 17). This was the same man who earlier was so depressed and discouraged that he questioned the Lord with his "... why ... where ... which ..." (Judges 6:13). What brought about the change? The Lord appeared unto him and looked upon him, and said, "Go ... save ... have not I sent thee?" (Judges 6:14). That look made all the difference, and Gideon became a strong, determined, courageous warrior for God. And now he could say to his little group, "Look on me, and do ...". With 301 dedicated souls, surrounded by broken pitchers and each man holding a trumpet and a lighted torch, the Lord defeated an enemy which was no doubt armed to the teeth.

What is the lesson here? We get discouraged just as Gideon did, and we begin to question and to doubt. Do we not need the Gideon experience? That look of encouragement from our glorious Leader, the Captain of our salvation (Hebrews 2:10, RV margin). We must be willing to carry on the fight with Him and for Him, and with the divine equipment He has given us. Let us not belittle that which He has given to us. Gideon's men did not question, complain, or doubt the battle plan, their fewness of numbers, or the scanty weapons. Nor should we. We must be prepared to blow our trumpets, break our pitchers, hold aloft our torches, and cry out, "victory ... through our Lord Jesus Christ" (1 Corinthians 15:57).

"Our glorious Leader claims our praise

For His own pattern given;

While the long cloud of witnesses

Show the same path to heaven."

FIFTY-FOUR: SEPARATION FROM THE WORLD (PART ONE)

Four apostles made reference to the world in their writings, and I have paraphrased their very weighty comments by way of introduction:

- James, in his most practical epistle, said that friendship with the world is enmity with God (James 4:4).
- Paul, who could have been considered worldly-wise before his conversion, counselled his fellow-Christians not to be conformed to this world (Romans 12:2).
- Peter, who had a very close view of the hatred of worldly men towards Christ, warns of corruption and defilement in the world (2 Peter 1:4; 2:20).
- John, the apostle of love, declares very firmly, "Love not the world, neither the things that are in the world" (1 John 2:15).

And what of the Lord and Master of these devoted men? He made it very clear that His kingdom and His disciples were not of the world, which hated them. In the world His followers must expect tribulation (John 16:33; 17:14; 18:36). There is a valid reason for the world to be considered in such an unfavourable light by the Lord and His apostles, and it is no doubt found in the revealing statement which He made as Calvary drew near. "I will no more speak much with you, for the prince of the world cometh: and he hath nothing in Me" (John 14:30). Are Christians fully aware of the importance of these words? They certainly add emphasis to the words of John that "the whole world lieth in the evil one" (1 John 5:19).

We are virtually being told that the course of this world is under the guidance and control of Satan. The seriousness of this revelation is even more emphasized by the Lord's temptation by the Devil in the wilderness. Taking Him up to a high mountain the adversary showed God's Son all the kingdoms of the world in a moment of time, saying, "To Thee will I give all this authority, and the glory of them: for it hath been delivered unto me; and to whosoever I will I give it" (Luke 4:6). This is an insight into the power the Devil has, and knowing that he is the controlling and guiding force behind the world's programmes and plans, how can Christians have affinity with them, or hold out the right hand of fellowship to the world?

It was indeed a black day when the ideal environment of the garden of Eden was invaded by Satan, the father of lies, for his foul treachery opened the floodgate of sinful pollution to engulf the human race until this day. High tide has not been reached even yet, and none but the blind can fail to see corruption, licentiousness, greed, violence and hatred mounting higher and higher until the climax is reached in the soon coming "last days". Having failed to gain the throne of heaven by rebellion (Isaiah 14:12-15), the adversary determined to rule the earth after he was cast out of the divine presence. There is great significance in the title the Lord Jesus gave him as "the prince of this world". It means the chief ruler.

The power of darkness is under the mastery of this potentate whose authority and influence and strength are superhuman. How thankful every Christian should be for the great work of the Saviour at Calvary which translated us from this evil power into the kingdom of God's dear Son (Colossians 1:13)! What a deliverance! But how alert we should be to the fact that the world is under Satan's sway, and although he is not all-powerful, as God alone is, yet he wields tremendous power, doing so until he is banished eternally to the lake of fire and brimstone (Revelation 20:10).

FIFTY-FIVE: SEPARATION FROM THE WORLD (PART TWO)

Until he is judged, "the god of this world" (2 Corinthians 4:4) will not only cause wickedness to increase, but he will use all the subtlety at his disposal to ensnare and entangle God's people in the multifarious involvements of this world. Obvious things, and apparently innocent things, will all be used to draw us into his net. The end in view is to render us impotent and useless for God. He will make the identical offer to us that he made to our Master, "all this will I give thee" if we will give him our time, our allegiance, our worship.

It was to disciples the Lord said, "For what shall a man be profited, if he shall gain the whole world, and forfeit his life?" (Matthew 16:26). How anxious the Devil is to draw us away from the Lord. Let us not then be deceived by the prosperity, the prospects and the pleasure the world has to offer. Let us get things into perspective by realizing that the world is getting worse, and is ripening fast for God's judgement. It is a good thing for Christians to keep a balance, having an "understanding of the times" like the children of Issachar (1 Chronicles 12:32); and then we will realize that we must stand aloof from a world which is a seething cauldron of immorality, witchcraft, cheating, gambling, conspiracies, drugs, alcoholism, filthy speech, lies, and greed. Ordinary people have little conception of how corrupt human society has become. Even a little lifting of the lid would shock beyond words any respectable human. How then can we make friends with this system, this society, this environment, which men have contrived and devised at the behest of the evil one?

We must face the fact, however, that we are in the world and we have a responsibility to live as lights, and act as pilgrims and strangers. We are in the world, but not of it, using but not abusing it (1 Corinthians 7:31). We cannot isolate ourselves from men, but we must insulate ourselves from those things which would compromise our position as those who have been brought "within a given circle" by God, which is one of the renderings of the word "peculiar" as describing His own people (1 Peter 2:9). Our citizenship is in heaven (Philippians 3:20), and this precludes us from involvement in the elections of governments. Our warfare is not against flesh and blood (Ephesians 6:12), and this prevents us from engaging in military combat. We are in the fellowship of God's Son (1 Corinthians 1:9), and so we cannot be joined to other fellowships. We are pilgrims and sojourners, and this would discourage us from gathering wealth and possessions as men do. This does not absolve us, of course, from so living as to meet our earthly obligations and to provide for our families.

But one of the seeming paradoxes of Scripture is that the Christian does not have to be negative in his approach to the world. We are reminded in an oft quoted verse, "For God so loved the world" (John 3:16), yet we are exhorted, "Love not the world" (1 John 2:15). A contradiction? No! God loved men and women; He loved sinners, but not their sin. And so He sent His Son who came into the world to save sinners (1 Timothy 1:15). It is incumbent upon us to love as Christ loved; not the things of the world, not the evil, not the pleasures, not the entertainment, not the things which the Devil uses to hold men in bondage. Our love should be for men and women who need Christ, and to be saved from eternal doom. The Eternal One who is the faithful and true Witness, wants us to be His witnesses (Acts 1:8); the One who said, "I am the light of the world" (John 9:5), tells us to "Let your light so shine before men" (Matthew 5:16). This is the Christian's positive approach to a world in darkness and in need.

> "Men die in darkness at your side,
>
> Without a hope to cheer the tomb,
>
> Take up the torch and wave it wide,
>
> The torch that lights time's thickest gloom."

FIFTY-SIX: FIFTY TIMES

Fifty! That is the number of visits paid by a Christian lady to a neighbouring husband and wife to invite them along to hear the gospel. And each time they refused. Did she give up? No! When she called the next time they reluctantly agreed to accompany her in the hope that she might be pacified and not ask them again. That night they were both saved. There was not only rejoicing in heaven among the angels of God, on that memorable night, but there was untold joy in the heart of that faithful, diligent worker for Christ.

One of the greatest endeavours of the enemy today is to discourage God's people. He is happiest when we are sad, depressed, despairing and ready to give up. Paul was well aware of this tendency when he wrote, "And let us not be weary in well-doing: for in due season we shall reap, if we faint not" (Galatians 6:9). To faint means to relax, to lose heart, to unloose (as a bow string). An arrow can only reach its mark from a taut bow and our service for the Master can only be its most effective when we rise above life's disappointments. Distributing leaflets can be one of the most discouraging aspects of gospel witness. Yet, unknown so often to the faithful scatterer of this precious seed, God is saving souls through a leaflet placed in a hand or in a home. A man was once saved from committing suicide through a Christian knocking on his door in order to give him personally a tract. He read the leaflet and was saved.

To be fainthearted carries the thought of being small of soul. We can actually shrink within ourselves. Our vision and interests can become almost microscopic instead of large and bountiful. Our energies become dissipated, our zeal wilts and defeat stares us in the face. This is when we are tempted to "throw in the towel". But in times like these there is very near to us a band of faithful witnesses, shouting to us their words of cheer. "Faint not", says Paul. "The joy of the LORD is your strength", declares Nehemiah (8:10). "The battle is the LORD's", cries David (1 Samuel 17:47). "Be of good courage", exclaims Ezra (10:4). "Hold fast", encourages Paul (1 Thessalonians 5:21). "Be thou faithful unto death, and I will give thee the crown of life", proclaims our Lord and Master (Revelation 2:10). And what shall we answer? "By Thy grace we will".

FIFTY-SEVEN: TWO OF YOU

Living in a world which is becoming more and more impersonal, and where computers and statistics are becoming more and more important, it is most encouraging to think of the Lord's personal interest in the ones and twos. It is surprising the number of times that He has used two things or two people to accomplish His purpose. He chose two sisters, Martha and Mary, to be His companions and to show Him loving care in their Bethany home (Luke 10:38). He chose two brothers, Moses and Aaron, to lead about three million captive Israelite men, women and children out of Egypt; an incomparable feat accomplished with a rod and the presence of God (Exodus 3:12; 4:29). He allowed two of His servants, Paul and Silas, to be unjustly cast into prison. Their limbs were fettered, but their tongues were not silent as they filled the night hours with prayers and singing. Heaven heard, souls were saved and a church of God blessed (Acts 16). Two unnamed spies were secretly hidden by Rahab after they came with the message of judgement for Jericho and of salvation for her house (Joshua 2:4). And in the counsels of the Sanhedrin, two men, Nicodemus and Joseph of Arimathaea, remained secretly hidden as disciples of Christ, until the Cross and the tomb brought them out into the open as friends of the Man of Calvary.

What shall we say of David and Jonathan, who excelled in brotherly love (2 Samuel 1:26); of Caleb and Joshua, the two in the minority who stood out for God against the tide of opposition, and alone among the men of war of that generation entered the land of promise-a reward for faithfulness (Numbers

14:30); of Aaron and Hur, those enduring men of strength who upheld the arms of Moses in a victorious attitude of prayer during the war with Amalek (Exodus 17:8-16)? "If two of you", says the Lord Jesus, "shall agree on earth as touching anything that they shall ask, 'it shall be done for them of My Father which is in heaven" (Matthew 18:19). Which two? Any two of you in a church of God. Two sisters; two brothers; a husband and wife; two overseers; two deacons; it matters not.

What does matter is the agreeing and the asking. Oh, that we might realize what God can do with two praying souls! Paul and Silas were answered in prison and the kingdom of God was extended. Aaron and Hur were honoured on a mountain top and victory resulted for Israel. Will not blessing come and victory be granted to us too, if, in the same spirit of faith and obedience we pray and faint not?

FIFTY-EIGHT: GREAT THINGS

A Christian widow was once commended for the many answers to prayer she had received. "You must have great faith in God", someone remarked to her. "'No", she replied, "faith in a great God". We do indeed have a great God, and when we consider the wonders of His creation, and the magnitude of His plan of salvation, we can truly exclaim, "How great Thou art!" So much of God's greatness is revealed in His word that we stand in awe. Some incidents show His holiness and others His majesty; yet again we see His grace and also His judgements. How sobering it is to read of a great white throne (Revelation 20:11) and a great gulf between saved and unsaved (Luke 16:26). But how marvellous to ponder the great peace found in His law (Psalm 119:165), and the great calm after the frightening storm on lake Galilee (Matthew 8:26). We can sit under His shadow with great delight (Song of Songs 2:3), and meditate on the Lord's return to this troubled earth in power and great glory (Matthew 24:30).

We can ponder the remnant days of that brave man Nehemiah, and the response of a grateful people of God with their great sacrifices and great joy (Nehemiah 12:43). And we can see God's way of preparing Moses for the great task of leading Israel from the bondage of Egypt, when showing him the burning bush that was not consumed. "I will turn aside now, and see this great sight, why the bush is not burnt", said Moses (Exodus 3:3). It was then God called unto him to "put off thy shoes from off thy feet, for the place whereon thou standest is holy ground" (vv.4,5). Moses was once a great man in the land of Egypt and no doubt he saw many great things, but none would compare with this experience in the desert. It has been said that his life was divided into three parts. He was forty years in Egypt learning to be something; forty years in the desert learning to be nothing; and forty years leading the children of Israel learning that God was everything.

We, too, have "great things" to occupy us. Worship and testimony are to be maintained in God's house where the Lord Jesus is Great High Priest (Hebrews 4:14) and Great Priest (10:21), and we look forward to this dispensation's end and the appearing of our great God and Saviour, Jesus Christ (Titus 2:13).

FIFTY-NINE: THE GOD OF THE VALLEYS

"Most discouraging ..." might easily have been the reaction of David, the courageous shepherd lad, as he faced Goliath, the well-armed giant in the vale of Elah. David had just left a trembling Israeli army, and a greatly disheartened king Saul. Now he was standing with sling in hand before a taunting, scornful behemoth of a man, who was armed to the teeth and being cheered on, no doubt, by an army with the scent of victory in their nostrils. There had been no cheering when David left the camp of Israel! But the brave son of Jesse, who had known the Lord's presence going through the valley of the shadow of death (Psalm 23), was to prove on this vital day that the LORD is a God of the valleys as well as a God of the hills. Victory came, not through sword and spear, but from a small stone. And so a despondent, defeated people were transformed into a victorious, pursuing army (1 Samuel 17).

"Most discouraging ..." could have been Nehemiah's reaction as he viewed, from the valley gate, the broken-down walls and flame-charred gates of Jerusalem. Before him, and a handful of faithful men, lay the gigantic task of restoring for God the ravages wrought by a relentless enemy. God's people had lived listlessly amongst the wastes of Jerusalem for years, and their morale was at its lowest. Held in the grip of discouragement amidst depressing desolation, the Jewish remnant seemed to be totally defeated. But Nehemiah, whose name means "the consolation of Jehovah", was not one to concede that the Lord is only a God of the hills and not of the valleys. Through virile action and encouraging words, he succeeded by God's help in rejuvenating the people unitedly to build, repair, and restore. "So the wall was finished" (Nehemiah 6:15), and later, "... all the people ... bowed their heads and worshipped" (Nehemiah 8:6).

"Most discouraging ...", too, can be our experiences today. But dare we endorse the claim of the Syrians that, "The LORD is a god of the hills, but He is not a god of the valleys" (1 Kings 20:28)? Of course not. Our God is unchanging and unfailing. He makes the valley of weeping a place of springs (Psalm 84:6); and provides valleys covered over with corn (65:13). Our valley experiences need not be those of despair and defeat for the God who gave David victory in the valley will surely do the same for us. "Lo I am with you alway" (Greek: 'all the days') (Matthew 28:20) is His promise.

SIXTY: THE BATTLE OF THE BEETLE

Insidiously it works away, boring at the hardest of wood, and leaving behind its tell-tale holes and powdered sawdust. Examination of the highest beams, and the oldest of wood, reveals its presence. The death watch beetle is most destructive, and it has been detected for years in Britain's House of Commons. Skilled craftsmen carry on a steady programme of cutting out and replacing ravaged sections with new wood. And so the battle of the beetle goes on constantly and continuously, almost like the believer's battle with sin in the flesh.

For it was just as silently and insidiously that sin bore its way into the life of Samson, the man of strength. Was he conscious of its destructive effect? Did he recognize the tell-tale marks, or had he become over-confident? Whatever the reason, we see him gradually losing the battle, and he had not even realized that the Lord had left him. Rapidly the enemy moved in. They put out his eyes, bound him, threw him into prison, and made him grind corn like oxen (Judges 16). Would any now recognize this pitiful figure as the man who had bodily removed the gates of a city, and had put an enemy army to flight? How devastating and desolating sin can be!

God in His grace and love, however, would not allow Samson to conclude his life in defeat. No doubt humbled in spirit by his broken link with heaven, and the ignominious treatment of his enemies, Samson's strength was restored by a faithful, merciful God, who never forgets a repentant soul. Jehovah Ropheka - the LORD who restores - is one of His titles (Psalm 23:3). It was a new Samson who was brought from the prison to entertain the enemy, but who ended up praying as he had never prayed before: "O Lord GOD, remember me ... strengthen me ... only this once" (Judges 16:28). What a prayer! God answered, and Samson brought the heathen temple down with a crash, slaying more in his death than in his life.

The same conflict which wore down Samson left its mark on David (2 Samuel 12:10,12), and was an anxiety to Paul (Romans 7:19,20), and can be our downfall, too. Our Christian lives can be eaten away so easily by anger, wrath, malice, railing, shameful speaking, lies, passion, evil desire, and covetousness (Colossians 3:5,8,9). Let these works of the flesh be cut out and replaced by the 'new wood' of love, joy, peace, longsuffering, kindness, goodness, faithfulness, meekness, and self-control (Galatians 5:22,23).

SIXTY-ONE: DAVID AND JONATHAN (PART ONE)

If we need a suitable example of how to live together in love and friendship, surely it's found in the kinship of David and Jonathan. Although so much bitterness, selfishness, pride and envy were in evidence all around them in the nation of Israel, there seemed to be a total lack of it in these two men who truly loved and respected each other. It is an impressive story of reciprocal love, true humility, anxious concern and sincere friendship. As the dark clouds of hatred and discontent swept across Israel's skies during the stormy reign of king Saul, the tender, unaffected relationship of David and Jonathan stood like a lighthouse, sending out its beams of unselfish devotion.

This story of the young prince and the young shepherd, has become a saga; but it is also a spiritual lesson of great import for us today. Did the apostle Paul have Jonathan, the heir-apparent of Israel, in mind when he wrote, "Love envieth not ... is not puffed up ... seeketh not its own" (1 Corinthians 13:4,5)? Perhaps not, but the divine qualities which Paul urged the Corinthians to reveal, were most certainly manifest by Jonathan towards David, who was later to become his brother-in-law. Humanly speaking, Jonathan was heir to the throne (1 Samuel 20:31), but instead of being absorbed by this ambition he was consumed by love for David, whom he considered to be the rightful heir (1 Samuel 23:17).

The reciprocal love of David and Jonathan flourished in an environment of adversity and opposition, and they did not allow these things to prevent it from becoming a lasting love which was to reveal itself in death and after death. What of our love for each other in churches of God? When Jonathan, one of Israel's most courageous warriors, fell with his brothers and kingly father, in battle with the Philistines, David lamented, "I am distressed for thee, my brother Jonathan: very pleasant hast thou been unto me: thy love to me was wonderful, passing the love of women" (2 Samuel 1:26).

There was later to surge up within David, when he became Israel's anointed king, a renewed wave of love for his dead friend, when he enquired, "Is there yet any that is left of the house of Saul, that I may show him kindness for Jonathan's sake" (2 Samuel 9:1)? And Mephibosheth, the helpless, neglected, crippled son of Jonathan, was found almost bereft, and certainly not in circumstances befitting the son of a prince, in Lo-debar, the place of no pasture. King David saw to it that the forgotten cripple was brought from poverty to plenty; from the beggar's table to the king's palace. All for Jonathan's sake. In this David manifested divine love, confirming the gracious tribute to him that he was a man after God's own heart.

And we, whose circumstances in a spiritual sense have paralleled those of Mephibosheth, have also exchanged our desolation and poverty in the place of no pasture, where sin brought us, for the King's table in the divine banqueting house; and over us is the banner of Christ's eternal love. Daily we should be thankful for the kindness of God shown towards us, for the sake of a greater than Jonathan, God's own dear Son.

SIXTY-TWO: DAVID AND JONATHAN (PART TWO)

When David slew Goliath, Jonathan did not resent the intrusion of this once obscure shepherd lad into the national limelight. Neither did he allow the subsequent jealousy and hatred of his father Saul towards David to influence him in any way. Saul was afraid of David (1 Samuel 18:12), but Jonathan, who had reason to fear his displacement by David as successor to the throne, loved him (18:3). Saul sought to kill the son of Jesse (18:11), but Jonathan strengthened David's hand in God (23:16). Saul devised mischief against David (23:9), but Jonathan spoke only good of him (19:4).

The self-abnegation and brotherly love of Jonathan are surely worthy of our imitation. What graciousness, kindness and friendship were shown by this man to the one who was going to replace his family as the royal line of Israel! His actions were contrary to what is expected of human nature, which seeks its own things first. They were more in keeping with divine nature as revealed by Christ, who pleased not Himself. Paul exhorted the Philippians to do nothing through vainglory, "but in lowliness of mind each counting other better than himself; not looking each of you to his own things, but each of you also to the things of others" (Philippians 2:3,4). This was the spirit of humility shown by Jonathan, who had as much reason as his father Saul to be chagrined by the increasing esteem of David amongst the people (1 Samuel 18:7). He was a man in touch with God (1 Samuel 14:10-12) and he bowed to the divine will and choice of David as Israel's king, thus restoring the royal line of Judah to its rightful place.

It should strengthen our hearts to see that adversity drew David and Jonathan closer together, as it should with us. The hatred and jealousy shown almost daily by Saul towards David intensified the dangers which surrounded the two friends, and Jonathan's loyalty based on their covenant of love (1 Samuel 18:3; 20:15,16; 23:18), never wavered. There was a long war between the house of Saul and the house of David (23:8), but Jonathan sought to be the peacemaker, an intensely valuable quality for all to imitate. There were times when he grieved for David (20:34), delighted in him, and endangered his life for him (19:1-7) and the love he showed must have compensated for what David apparently did not receive from his own brothers. There were some in Israel who were to say, "Thine are we, David, and on thy side" (1 Chronicles 12:18), but Jonathan had said this in his heart long before on the memorable day when the souls of the two young men were knit together in love. Jonathan's vision was filled with the vale of Elah when David jeopardized his life in the battle to defeat Goliath, and his triumph brought peace and salvation to Israel. His love and loyalty for David were born that day, and he was to strip off his princely robe, his sword, bow, and girdle, and give them to David. This acknowledgement of David as Israel's king he confirmed later in another covenant of love (1 Samuel 20:12-23).

In his lifetime, David was to experience often the loyalty and love of others like Abigail, Ittai, and his mighty men. But none, it seems, could compare with the love of Jonathan, that love which shared dangers unto death, suffered long, obliterated self, and surpassed the tenderest of all human love, the love of women. It is such a love that our King, a greater than David, expects of us. Jonathan saw the battle and victory of Elah, and pledged his very life to the great victor David. We have seen by faith the battle and victory of Calvary with its eternal consequences, won by Christ, the eternal Lover of our souls. Are our souls knit to Him? Are we facing with Him daily the adversities, the trials and problems of life? Jonathan gave his all for David. What is our answer to the Lord's enquiry, "I gave My life for thee; what hast thou given for Me"?

> "Oh, let my life be given,
>
> My years for Thee be spent;
>
> World fetters all be riven,
>
> And joy with suffering blent.
>
> What Thou hast done for me
>
> Demands my all for Thee."

SIXTY-THREE: OVER THERE

The boat was slowly moving down one of China's main rivers, and the aged missionary aboard with his son seemed to be talking to himself. "It is over there, I know, but I cannot see very well", he remarked, peering through almost blind eyes to a familiar place in the distance. "Over there" was the scene of his many meetings with God; the place he resorted to in times of crisis and discouragement. This was his Peniel, or his place of the bush, where unforgettable experiences happened, and the soul grasped afresh the precious promises of an Eternal God.

The Christian must never cease to marvel at the grace of the King of Eternity who delights to meet with men and women. Oh, the wonder of it all! A mere man, perhaps considered of no account by earthly kings and dignitaries, enjoying audience with heaven's King. Jacob met Him at Peniel, and He blessed him there (Genesis 32:22-32). It was an unforgettable night of wrestling, and in the morning he was greeted by the glory and brightness of the rising sun, as he limped along the road over Peniel (v.31). Jacob was a limping man for the rest of his life, but he would never forget seeing "God face to face" (v.30). That limp might have a spiritual lesson for those of us who long for great experiences with the God of Jacob, for it is indicative of the life of faith which is taken a step at a time.

Moses met Him at the burning bush, where he was privileged to hear God calling unto him (Exodus 3:4). Unlike Jacob, Moses "hid his face; for he was afraid to look upon God" (v.6). This memorable meeting resulted in the man, who had fled from Egypt, returning there to lead to freedom over three million Israelites, to a divinely chosen place where they could serve and worship God. The Psalmist met Him at the little mountain of Mizar (Psalm 42:6). Only once is this place mentioned in Scripture, but it was a place of remembrances. Was it here the cast down soul was uplifted and strengthened, the sad countenance made to rejoice, and the tears of sorrow were wiped away? Whatever the experience, it is made memorable by its mention.

And what a meeting place the Emmaus road proved to be when two downcast disciples met the Lord; where they walked and talked with Him, and heard Him speak, and were privileged to look full into His wonderful face. Their hearts burned within them after listening to His refreshing ministry, and they were quick to tell others of their memorable experience (Luke 24).

But greatest of all meetings will surely be "in the air", when our blessed Lord Jesus returns with a shout, the voice of the archangel, and the trump of God (1 Thessalonians 4). No limping then, for we shall all be changed; no fears, no tears, no downcast souls, for we shall be happy to see His glorious face. We, who were once sinners, will be made ready for His presence, and we shall spend all eternity with Him. What a memorable meeting that will be! May the Lord's coming to make such a meeting possible, not be delayed. Even so come, Lord Jesus.

SIXTY-FOUR: LISTEN!

Did you know that on an average day people spend more time listening than they do speaking? It is the claim of experts in the field of verbal and written communication that 45% of an average day is spent in listening, 30% in speaking, 16% in reading, and 9% in writing. It is startling to realize, at times, that we have all been taught to speak, both at home and at school, but few have been instructed in the art of listening.

There was a time when we enjoyed the song of the bird, the beauty of the flower, and the wonder of the blue sky, which were all reminders of the great Creator who became our Saviour. But we now seem to have so little time to listen, to see and to read. The result can only be detrimental to our natural and spiritual lives. We must learn to quieten our souls (Psalm 131:2), and hear God speaking to us. "Be still", He says, "and know that I am God" (Psalm 46:10), and we must listen. "Sit still", Naomi said to Ruth, "until thou know how the matter will fall" (Ruth 3:18). Ruth listened, and she saw God's purpose unfold in her life. "Stand ye still, and see the salvation of the LORD", was the message to king Jehoshaphat, and because he listened the enemy were defeated while the people were singing and praising the LORD (2 Chronicles 20:22). By listening the king also heard these assuring words, "Fear not, nor be dismayed ... for the LORD is with you" (v.17).

Listening to God through His word will bring its blessing and encouragement to us. "Blessed are they that hear the word of God, and keep it", said the Lord to the multitude (Luke 11:28). Why? Paul might provide the answer in his warning to the

Corinthian saints. "There are ... so many kinds of voices in the world", he wrote, "and no kind is without signification" (1 Corinthians 14:10). Some voices would tell us today that we should be experiencing the spectacular, or the "charismatic", as it is described, despite what the word of God has to say. But when the three disciples saw the Lord transfigured on the mount, and Peter wanted to make three tabernacles, God spoke from a cloud saying, "This is My Son, My Chosen: hear ye Him" (Luke 9:35). He wanted them to listen. He did not want them to get things out of balance. After the scene they had witnessed had disappeared, there was still the need to listen to His Son. When Moses saw the wilderness spectacle of the burning bush that was not consumed, God called to him. He wanted Moses to listen. Again, the scene of the bush would pass away, but the Lord would still be speaking, and unless Moses hearkened to the instructions for the deliverance of the captive Israelites, then God's purposes might be frustrated.

Listening to God's voice, and being obedient to it, is what God wants from us. The human race would have been saved much grief if Eve had listened to the Lord rather than to the enemy. So shall we. We live in a world of ceaseless activity, but we must not let it reduce our ability to listen effectively. Our spiritual health depends on listening to God's word and obeying it. "Hear, and your soul shall live" (Isaiah 55:3).

SIXTY-FIVE: WHATEVER HAPPENED TO THE BRASS SNAKE?

The answer to that question is that it ended up as one of the broken things of Scripture. For hundreds of years it had remained with the children of Israel, but when Hezekiah found the people were burning incense to it, he broke it into pieces (2 Kings 18:1-8). To him it was only a piece of brass (v.4, RV margin), which was a true estimation. It had served its purpose in the past when the Israelites were bitten by fiery serpents in the wilderness, and they were told to look at it and be healed. Its purpose for the future as typified in the Lord Jesus (John 3) was fulfilled in His death at Calvary. It had no specific use in Hezekiah's reign, unless as a reminder of the grace and power of God. But when it became an object of worship, it was destroyed by this faithful man of God.

Hezekiah was a good man. There are seven commendable things said about him in 2 Kings 18. He did that which was right in the eyes of the Lord (v.3); he destroyed the idols, and the places where they were worshipped (v.4); he trusted the Lord (v.5); there was none like him among all the kings of Judah (v.5); he clave to the Lord (v.6); he kept His commandments (v.6); he prospered because the Lord was with Him (v.7). How different from the people over whom he reigned! He would have no part in their high places, the Asherah and graven images; rather he sought to lead them in the way of the Lord.

It is remarkable how far the people of God can drift. I heard recently of a Christian woman attending a seance, and attempting to reach her dead Christian husband through a spiritist medium. How can a Christian succumb to such suggestions? It certainly emphasizes to us the subtlety of the prince of the power of the air (Ephesians 2:2), who is also the prince of this world (John 14:30). We live in a day when demon worship, spiritism and occult practices are spreading rapidly amongst young people and unwary adults. Paul warned of "later times" when some would fall away from the faith, giving heed to seducing spirits, and doctrines of demons (1 Timothy 4:1). He told of young widows who turned aside after Satan (5:15). They went from house to house as tattlers and busybodies, speaking things they ought not (v.13). This was perhaps more serious than we realize for the Greek word for busybody is also used for the "curious arts" mentioned in Acts 19:19.

Christians should be warned that there are things taking place today that we should shun, and not attempt to dabble in them. The reading of teacups, the so-called telling of fortunes, the consulting of horoscopes, the apparently innocent "magic tricks", can arouse a curiosity which might lead into the more serious realm of forbidden things. We should be aware of reports which indicate that in the USA alone there are ten million adherents to the occult arts connected with witchcraft and Satan worship; that the first Satanic bible has been published; and that there is a first Church of Satan in existence. Let us then avoid even the remotest association with such things. Let us rather hold fast to that which is good (1 Thessalonians 5:21), the appeal made to a people who turned to God from idols, to serve a living and true God, and to wait for His Son from heaven (1 Thessalonians 1:9,10).

SIXTY-SIX: SHOW ME A TOKEN

A rainbow, a scarlet cord and a fleece are some of the tokens revealed in Scripture to indicate the faithfulness of God. "Show me a token for good," said David (Psalm 86:17), and his prayer no doubt finds an echo in our hearts as we seek to see the hand of God in our lives. There is a possibility that some of us might have avoided much trouble and disappointment in our Christian experience if we had sought and received a token from the Lord instead of following our own plans and ideas. The idea is prevalent among men that our actions should be based on our own intuition and reasoning, but the child of God is only on a sure foundation when he has a word from the Lord; and so we pray, "Show me a token for good."

Gideon, the mighty man of valour, who was sent by the Lord to save Israel, took time to obtain a divine token before entering the fray against Midian and Amalek (Judges 6:33-40). He sought it firstly in the wet fleece upon the dry ground, and then in the dry fleece upon the wet ground, "... and God did so ..." It was only when he accepted the further sign that God Himself proposed for his assurance, that Gideon was prepared to go forward with the small army of three hundred men to put the enemy to flight. Humanly speaking, everything about Gideon bespoke frailty. Three companies of one hundred apiece; empty pitchers with torches; trumpets and a challenging shout; could he defeat the mighty enemy by these, alone? Yes, he put them to flight, because as the Lord through Paul said later that He "chose the weak things of the world, that He might put to shame the things that are strong."

It could be that we would gain more victories in our battles for Him if only we would wait for His tokens. We are just as frail as Gideon and his three hundred men. In 2 Corinthians 4:6,7 Paul speaks of earthen vessels which contain the treasure of "the light of the knowledge of the glory of God in the face of Jesus Christ". The vessels speak of you and me, and the word "earthen" indicates how fragile we are, and as easily broken as the pitchers of Gideon's men: this in order that the divine light might shine forth from us. It is the "fragile vessel" that proves that the power is of God, and not of ourselves (verse 7).

From Rahab, the prostitute, we can learn what a token can be. Knowing the power of God manifested on Israel's behalf, she pleaded with the spies to save her and her family when Jericho was attacked (Joshua 2:1-24). She said, "Swear unto me by the LORD, since I have dealt kindly with you that ye also will deal kindly with my father's house, and give me a true token."

The token was a line of scarlet thread, which she bound in the window as a token of the covenant. In the days of Noah, after God had purged the earth in judgement by water, He placed a token in the sky. To Noah He said, "This is the token of the covenant which I make between Me and you and every living creature" (Genesis 9:12). The Lord could not have chosen a more conspicuous place to manifest to all the evidence of His future grace! Every time we see the rainbow we are reminded of God's token for good, but He also looks upon the token of His everlasting covenant. The Lord has used His tokens in the past. Let us each pray, "Lord, show me a token for good."

SIXTY-SEVEN: LONELINESS

It is no respector of persons. The young, the middle-aged, and the aged have all known loneliness as an undesirable companion. Surely there is nothing worse than the waves of deep depression and despair which sweep over one at such times; or the feeling of having been deserted, or of not having a friend in the world. One can know the experience in a crowd, or within the confines of a tiny room. Some know it only occasionally, while others experience the grimness of prolonged loneliness. None of us would seek it intentionally, and it is only those who have felt the trauma that can fully appreciate the indescribable sadness that lonely people have to endure.

But let us remember as Christians that there is a difference between being alone and being lonely. It is a good thing to enjoy the quietness and the peace which comes from God as we seek His help to sort out the confusions, anxieties and troubles which life brings. In such circumstances we might be alone, but not lonely. The Lord is there with us in the circumstances, and He is fulfilling the promise of His presence. "I will in no wise fail thee, neither will I in any wise forsake thee", is His assurance (Hebrews 13:5). Is this something we have forgotten, and so we are overcome by our feelings because we think we are on our own battling things out? Perhaps Gideon thought the same. How depressed and lonely he seemed to be. But what a difference when he realized that the Lord was at hand. The questioning why, where and wherewith (Judges 6:13), were all changed by the Lord's comforting word, "Surely I will be with thee" (v.16). A discouraged Gideon became a mighty man of valour.

Moses, anxious and lonely, after his hasty flight from Egypt, needed to be reassured by the Lord, "Certainly I will be with thee" (Exodus 3:12). This is what he needed before returning to the land of his birth, to lead out triumphantly the Lord's captive people. And what of David, who must have known much loneliness, in his oft flights from the hateful king Saul, and felt himself hunted as a partridge upon the mountains? He has passed on to us the wonderful words of courage, "Yea, though I walk through the valley of the shadow of death, I will fear no evil; for Thou art with me" (Psalm 23:4). Before the Lord returned to heaven He said to His disciples, "Lo, I am with you alway" (Matthew 28:20). We are not to feel at any time that we are doing His work on our own, or that our Christian walk is a lonely one, for it is written in connection with the two downcast disciples on the road to Emmaus, "Jesus Himself drew near, and went with them" (Luke 24:15). A 93-year-old Christian once commented to me: "At my age people say that life gets lonely. Not so with me. I know the nearness of His presence in my room, and I can talk to Him". Amen.

SIXTY-EIGHT: UNTIL...

In the Song of Songs we have this lovely stanza: "Until the day be cool, and the shadows flee away, I will get me to the mountain of myrrh, and to the hill of frankincense" (4:6). Our thoughts and meditations of Christ can be most sweet as we ascend in a spirit of reverence the mountain of myrrh, where He "bare our sins in His body upon the tree" (1 Peter 2:24). We behold His torn brow and bleeding back, pierced hands and feet, and wounded side; and to our awe-struck soul there come afresh the words, so deeply personal and penetrating, "... My body ... given for you ... My blood ... for you" (Luke 22:19,20).

The One who loved us and gave Himself for us, longs for our remembrance of Him. What unspeakable joy it would be if the Lord descended from heaven and called us to Himself at a time when we were "breaking bread at His command"! Our hearts should be tuned to this possibility, as the keeping of the Breaking of the Bread is only "till He come", "Until the day be cool, and the shadows flee away". Paul says, "For as often as ye eat this bread, and drink the cup, ye proclaim the Lord's death till He come (1 Corinthians 11:26). How vital and important is this proclamation, for it is to saint and to sinner. It declares to all "that Christ died for our sins ... and that He was buried and that He hath been raised on the third day according to the Scriptures" (1 Corinthians 15:3,4).

There are many mountains mentioned in God's word, but to the Christian Calvary excels them all. This "mountain of myrrh" tells of His perfect sacrifice in death, while the "hill of frankincense" tells of His perfect life. What a contrast between the two! The one with its poignant vision of suffering grief and shame; the other with its precious view of that fragrant and holy life which men admired and with which God was so well pleased. There never has been, or can be a, life like His. Ponder the fourfold testimony to His holiness: His Father declared, "This is My beloved Son in whom I am well pleased" (Matthew 3:17), an unclean spirit said, "Thou art the Holy One of God" (Mark 1:24), Pilate said, "I ... find no fault in this Man" (Luke 23:14), and the Roman centurion affirmed, "Certainly this was a righteous Man" (Luke 23:47).

There is much to think about in this busy life, but a rich field of meditation has been left for us, as we quietly contemplate the fragrant, sinless life of the Son of God and the sweet savour of His meritorious death.

May we as God's people recover the art of musing upon Him despite all the demands made upon us, and the activity going on around us. A threefold experience of rich blessing awaits each one of us - to ascend the hill of frankincense, the mountain of myrrh, and the hill of the Lord (Psalm 24:3). May we do so in spirit and in truth, remembering that it may be very soon that the dawn of His coming shall break, and as the shadows flee away we shall see Him whom our souls love. "The voice of My Beloved! behold He cometh" (Song of Songs 2:8).

SIXTY-NINE: EPITAPHS (PART ONE)

God has recorded in the Scriptures His epitaphs of men and women, some of which are good, and some bad. David, for example, is described twice in Nehemiah as a "man of God" (12:24,36). Is there a higher tribute that could be paid to a mortal? Should we not so live that after our departure it might be said of us, too, that "he was a man of God", or "she was a woman of God". Linked with David in this great commendation is Timothy. "Thou ... man of God, Paul writes to him, "follow after righteousness, godliness, faith, love, patience, meekness" (1 Timothy 6:11). This is the only time the expression is used in the New Testament, which emphasizes even more the value of its tribute.

Both David and Timothy revealed their human weaknesses, for men are only men at their best; but the purpose of their lives was to be men of God. They lived in the conscious knowledge of what was expected of them; they set a goal and sought to reach it. When they were weak, they sought His strength; when they stumbled, they reached out for His hand; in companionship they walked with Him; in friendship they shared with Him their innermost thoughts; Him they worshipped, and to Him they prayed; and so the characteristics of the divine One became manifest in their lives, and it was evident to others that they were men of God.

The references to David as a man of God associate him with praise and thanksgiving. This is indeed a great example for us today, for there is ever the need for men of God who are able to lead in, and share with God's people, thanksgiving and praise, and the making of melody in our hearts with psalms, hymns, and spiritual songs. What greater epitaph could we desire than this?

SEVENTY: EPITAPHS (PART TWO)

The life of Saul is a striking contrast to that of David. Saul was a king with poor judgement, and a man who made many mistakes which might have been avoided. After being victorious over him in the last battle of his life, the enemy found Saul and his three sons slain on the battlefield of Mount Gilboa. Cutting off his head, the gloating Philistines sent it around their country as evidence of Saul's ignominious defeat; his body they hung from the ramparts of Beth-shan; and his armour (was it the same armour that David refused to wear in his fight against Goliath?) adorned the temple of idols in Ashtaroth. What an end to Israel's king! What a grim epitaph without words! It is left to gracious David to pay a lamenting tribute to Saul and his son Jonathan. "... The bow of Jonathan turned not back, and the sword of Saul returned not empty ... lovely and pleasant in their lives, and in their death they were not divided" (2 Samuel 1:22,23). The end of Saul was so different from that of David who died "full of days, riches, and honour" (1 Chronicles 29:28), an epitaph any might covet.

And what shall we say of Abraham, the friend of God; of Moses, the meekest man in all the earth; and of Paul, who fought the good fight, finished the course, and kept the faith. Wonderful epitaphs indeed to men who loved their God, but we must not forget the worthy women who received their praise from God also. There is a beautiful epitaph to Dorcas, one of the early disciples, who was "full of good works and almsdeeds which she did" (Acts 9:36); and of the silent woman, who poured her cruse of oil over the Master's head. He said "Wheresoever the gospel shall be preached throughout the whole world, that also which this woman hath done shall be spoken of for a memorial of her" (Mark 14:9); Phoebe was a succourer of many (Romans 16:2), and Priscilla (with her husband Aquila) placed her life in jeopardy for Paul (v.4); and we are given the names of three wonderful women who during the Lord's life on earth performed the unpopular service in that day of ministering unto the Master and His disciples, of their substance (Luke 8:2,3).

Against the brightness of these testimonies are cast the dark shadows of those like Demas, who forsook Paul and the churches for the world's applause; of Solomon, whose heart was turned to idolatry with all its evils; and king Uzziah, who was cut off from the house of the LORD to live in an isolated house, and died a leper (2 Chronicles 26). What warnings these are to us today! If we had a sudden homecall, what epitaph would we leave behind? Have we been found faithful, gracious, loving, kind, full of good works? What will men say of us? More important still, what is God recording about us?

Did you love *Light From Darke*? Then you should read *The View From Goak Hill: A Christian's Perspective on Life and Living* by Gilbert Grierson!

Gilbert's life changed when he came to know Jesus in Israel in 1975: "God opened my eyes to see truth that brought me peace and hope. Now I look at the world differently. These writings are my attempt to pass on what I see from my "Goak Hill" to ordinary people like myself who are troubled about the world we live in and are looking for answers".

A potter and former hospice nurse, Gilbert combines Bible verses and some of his everyday experiences to draw out some challenging and encouraging life lessons for a journey through life with Jesus.

About the Publisher

Hayes Press (www.hayespress.org) is a registered charity in the United Kingdom, whose primary mission is to disseminate the Word of God, mainly through literature. It is one of the largest distributors of gospel tracts and leaflets in the United Kingdom, with over 100 titles and hundreds of thousands despatched annually.

Hayes Press also publishes Plus Eagles Wings, a fun and educational Bible magazine for children, six times a year and Golden Bells, a popular daily Bible reading calendar in wall or desk formats.

Also available are over 100 Bibles in many different versions, shapes and sizes, Christmas cards, Christian jewellery, Eikos Bible Art, Bible text posters and much more!

22540208R00093

Printed in Great Britain
by Amazon